Jean Racine

Jean Racine

KARL VOSSLER

Translated by Isabel and Florence McHugh

Frederick Ungar Publishing Co.
New York

Translated from the German *Jean Racine* by Karl Vossler

Library of Congress Catalog Card Number: 68-25899

Printed in Hungary
ISBN: 0-8044-2951

Contents

1 *Racine's Character and Life* 7

2 *The Man and His Time* 23

3 *Racine's Works* 35

Their Special Nature 35
Their Value 42
The Individual Dramas 44

LA THÉBAÏDE 44
ALEXANDRE LE GRAND 48
ANDROMAQUE 49
LES PLAIDEURS 54
BRITANNICUS and BAJAZET 57
BÉRÉNICE 61
MITHRIDATE and IPHIGÉNIE 71
PHÈDRE 76
ESTHER 85
ATHALIE 92

Les Cantiques Spirituels 101

4 *Tragic Drama from Euripides to Racine* 105

5 *Racine's Rhetorical and Poetic Art* 119

Chronological Table 137

Racine's Life 137

Racine's Works 138

Notes 141

Index 151

1 Racine's Character and Life

One does not have to know much about Racine's life in order to understand his literary work. The latter is transparently clear; the former by no means so. Racine was not a strong and powerful character, but his nature was one of immeasurable depth. The factors and influences of nationality, race, and period that fashioned and formed him were so inexhaustible and so conflicting that he could express them only in literature, but was almost overwhelmed by them in life.

When we follow the course of his life, we note that Racine seems always to have been trying to escape from himself. He worked out his artistic destiny with a bad conscience, as if it were sinful. At the age of thirty-seven, having reached the height of his literary powers and also the zenith of his stage success, he renounced dramatic composition, for which he must surely have felt himself uniquely fitted, and changed his whole way of living, devoting himself from then on solely to his family, to the Christian community, and to the service of the state under Louis XIV. And it took nothing less than the request—in fact, the command—of the sovereign himself to induce the eccentric fugitive from the muses to produce a few more dramas for the court and some religious works. When Racine learned that a young Jesuit had denounced his tragedies in a sermon, he wrote to Boileau, his most faithful friend: "As for my tragedies, I surrender them willingly to his criticism. For a long time past, God has given me the grace to care little for the good or the ill that can be said of them, and to concern myself only with the account that I shall have to render Him one day."[1] He frequently and forcibly warns his eldest son against occupying himself with either creating or enjoying literature, against reading novels and visiting the theater and the opera, for all these lead to dissipation of the mental powers and disfavor in the sight of God.[2]

Undoubtedly the attitudes of the time, social and moral considerations, and, above all, Racine's Jansenist upbringing contributed much to this renunciation of his theatrical vocation; but a person at once stronger and less complicated would have been able to withstand influences of this kind and remain faithful to his genius, as the examples of Corneille and Molière show.

True, Jean Racine's will was not weak, but it was pliant; it bent before worldly as before heavenly powers, shunned strong resistance and dangerous enemies, and sought its internal and external well-being in familiar waters rather than swim against the current or allow itself to be driven downstream. In both temporal and eternal things this was an essentially diplomatic rather than a militant nature. "One must be regular with regular people, just as I have always been a wolf with you and your comrades the other wolves," he wrote to La Fontaine in a humorous letter of his youth (November 11, 1661),[3] and with this jest he betrays to us the secret of his life. People like him probably never blurt out the secrets of their souls when writing seriously; for this reason the lighthearted and playful utterances of his youth are much more illuminating than are the thoughtful writings and actions of his manhood.

He certainly never was frivolous and high-spirited in the full sense of these words. How could he have been? As an orphan reared by his grandparents and brought up in the fear of the Lord in stern institutions and with that practical, rigid, unadorned, and therefore somewhat joyless Christian love cultivated by the Jansenists, the character of the imaginative boy was inevitably and all too early warped and bent to the hypocritical art of hiding and dissembling. His youngest son, Louis Racine, tells a significant story of his father's school days in Port Royal. "My father chanced to find the Greek novel by Heliodoros about the love of Theagenes and Chariclea. He devoured it, but was caught in the act by the sacristan Claude Lancelot, who tore the book out of his hand and flung it into the fire. My father found ways and means of procuring another copy, which met with the same fate, whereupon he felt obliged to buy a third. And in order to have no further fear of confiscation, he memorized it, then brought it to the sacristan, saying, 'You can burn this one too.'"[4]

Indeed, the watchfulness of his educators extended even beyond the school years, and with it the necessity of cloaking his scandalous literary tastes. On September 13, 1660, he wrote to the gallant Abbé Le Vasseur, the most intimate of his accomplices: "I was just about to consult, as Malherbe did,[5] an old servant in our home to make sure of my judgment, only I perceived that she is Jansenist like her master,[6] and that she could betray me: and that would be my complete ruin, seeing that every day I still receive letter upon letter, or to be more correct, excommunication upon excommunication, because of my unfortunate sonnet. Thus I have been obliged to refer to myself alone regarding the quality of my verses."[7]

It would be mistaken to conclude from the light tone of such utterances that his secrecies and arts of dissimulation were any particular pleasure to him. He employed them only as a sort of self-defense and in the depressing consciousness of his own weakness; otherwise he was anything but deceitful or hypocritical. When living with his uncle, Sconin, the vicar-general of the bishop in Uzès, with a view to taking holy orders for the sake of a benefice, he was not really happy: "It is surely bad enough to play the hypocrite here without doing so also in Paris by letters; for I call it hypocrisy to write letters in which one must speak only of devotion and do nothing but commend oneself to others' prayers. It is not that I do not need them; but I would wish that people would pray for me without my being obliged to request it so much. If God wills that I shall become prior, I shall do as much praying for others as they will have done for me."[8]

I do not even find any indication that he was at all inclined to jocose lies, roguish hoaxing, or teasing deceptions. An adroit man of the world and shrewd business executive,[9] he felt all untruthfulness to be a burdensome armor that he had to don in case of need, and that he was able to wear with unobtrusive grace, but that he immediately discarded within the circle of proven friends. For he yearned for naturalness, genuine humanity, trust, and friendship. "*Nihil mihi nunc scito tam deesse quam hominem eum quicum omnia quae me ad aliqua afficiunt una communicem, qui me amet, qui sapiat, quicum ego colloquar, nihil fin-aam, nihil dissimulem, nihil obtegam. Non homo, sed littus, atque aer, et solitudo mera. Tu autem qui saepissime curam et angorem animi mihi in rebus omnibus conscius et omnium meorum sermonum et consiliorum particeps esse solebas, ubinam es?* If Cicero had been at Uzès as I am, and you had been in the place of his friend Atticus, would he have been able to speak otherwise?"[10] He wrote thus to his friend Le Vasseur after half a year of separation.

In friendship he was even more reliable than in enmity, for he needed moral support and dialogue as he did his daily bread, and in difficult situations he needed guidance and advice as well. He clung with unconditional fidelity to his literary and moral mentor Boileau-Despréaux. Never did one shadow of mistrust cloud this bond that lasted thirty-six years.[11] When Boileau came to his deathbed he embraced him, saying: "How lucky I am to be permitted to die in your presence!"[12] Few have felt more keenly that the most precious thing on earth is the affection and help of one's fellows. He was a modest, genial, and lovable companion. To his son he writes: "If I dare cite my own example to you, I would tell you that one of the things that has done me most good is to have spent my youth in the society of people who were willing to speak the truth to one another, and who hardly spared each other in regard to their faults; and I took a good deal of care to correct those they found in me, which were very numerous indeed, and which would have made it very difficult for me to get on with people in the intercourse of the world."[13]

Nature and landscape meant little to him, but human relations—manners, customs, and conventions, the written and unwritten laws of the family, the state, the Church, society, mutual services and agreements—were extremely important to him. For these values he had an uncommonly sensitive feeling, a scrupulous conscience, and devout reverence. It goes without saying that, like every strongly individual character, every highly original mind, he encountered much trouble and pain in making himself fit in with the complicated organizations of human society. Having embarked while still a child on a course of dissimulation, evasion, and compromise, he could hardly be expected to rebel against society in principle. Given Racine's unprotesting disposition, any rebelliousness could only have amounted to friction and disharmony of a personal kind, to passing vexation and anger. The most famous case of this is the disagreement with Port-Royal, which is worth relating briefly. The disapproval, sometimes tacit and sometimes loudly expressed, with which the literary efforts, theatrical experiments, and pursuits, from which he expected fame and fortune, were regarded by his Jansenist relatives, teachers, and friends, oppressed him from an early age. One day, apparently in 1663, he received from his aunt, Sœur Agnès de Sainte-Thècle, of Port-Royal, a letter concerning his dealings with actors and actresses: "I write this to you in the bitterness of my heart and with tears in my eyes. . . . I have learned, to my grief, that you are more than ever frequenting the company of persons whose name is abominable to all those who have any piety, however little, and with reason, since they are forbidden entry to the Church and to the communion of the faithful, even at the hour of death, unless they repent. You can judge, then, my dear nephew, of the anguish I am suffering, since you are not ignorant of the love I have always borne you, you know that I have never desired anything else for you than that you should be completely devoted to God in some honest employment. I therefore beseech you, my dear nephew, to have pity on your soul, and to reclaim your heart and consider seriously the abyss into which you have thrown yourself. I shall ask this grace of God for you. I wish that what has been told me of you were not true. But if you are so unfortunate as not to have broken off associations which dishonor you in the eyes of God and man, you must not think of coming to see us, for you know well that I could not speak to you, knowing you to be in a state so deplorable and so opposed to Christianity. . . ."[14]

Apparently the budding poet and worldling received similar affectionate scolding almost daily at this time—excommunication upon excommunication, as he called them with wry humour! The first successes at the court and in the theater—his *Thébaïde* and *Alexandre*—helped him to forget all this. But when, on December 31, 1665, his former teacher, Pierre Nicole, the famous grammarian and theologian of Port-Royal, published a pamphlet, *Lettres sur l'hérésie imaginaire,* in which he called the authors of novels and plays "public poisoners of souls and spiritual murderers," Racine's patience broke down. Although Nicole was not directly attacking him, but rather the sensational man of letters Des Marets de Saint-Sorlin, he wrote and published—anonymously—a reply[15] full of elegant fury, venomous wit, and enlightened worldliness, which by its grace and cleverness won the finest scholars of the capital to his side and brought public ridicule to the solemnity of the Jansenists, the mentality of his benefactors, and in fact the faith of his childhood and his later years. This letter is a curiosity as a literary and personal polemic, but in practical content it is an unmanly product of ill-considered petulance. That it was only momentary irritation—not any consciously responsible conviction, or distress of conscience, or even indignation—that sharpened his pen is clear from the fact that one word from Boileau sufficed to make him cease the quarrel. He had already composed a second rejoinder to two replies from the Jansenist side, and had shown this to Boileau. But when the latter said to him, "That is very nicely written, but you do not realize that you are writing against the best people in the world," he threw it back into the drawer.[16] And later, when the Abbé Tallemant reminded him, before the Academy, of this youthful polemic, he is said to have cried: "Yes, Monsieur, you are right: that is the most shameful thing in my life, and I would give all my blood to efface it."[17] The Frenchman's love of anecdotes may have added a little more point to the facts; nevertheless it remains clear that even at the time of his break with Port-Royal, Racine had no wish to make decisions on principle or to define clearly the position of Christianity regarding the secular arts and pastimes that were so important to him. It is also clear that his disagreement with the Jansenists, as the most conscientious representatives of Catholic spirituality, was only a personal quarrel, and in no way a matter of faith or conviction, or even of the philosophy of art. In no way did he regard those letters against the Jansenists as the essential point of the question at issue, and he avoided this essential point with the adroitness of a diplomat practiced in compromise, however persistently his opponent pointed to it. "What do you expect? Not everyone is capable of devoting himself to such important things; not everyone can write against the Jesuits. There is more than one route leading to fame."[18]

After he had conquered fame in *his* way, and tasted its hollowness, he longed for reconciliation with Port-Royal. After years of estrangement from them and of total absorption in creative literary work, he allowed Boileau to lead him back to his friends and teachers in Port-Royal. No great difficulties can have lain in the way of the much-discussed "conversion," which was really a natural return home, for on both sides only passionate outbursts and words had to be forgiven; no change of convictions was called for.[19]

Whenever he had offended against existing and generally recognized customs, opinions, or institutions, Racine always admitted he had been wrong, and this happened as soon as the first outburst of passion was over. He was a fundamentally modest person who did not rely on self-glorification, and he hated the vanity of the individual mind—in other words, pseudo-intellectual "smartness"—just as much as he hated pride. "Shall we always seek cleverness in the things that demand it the least?" he asks.[20] All trifling, all individualistic side-stepping, died away with the passing of his youth, just as the lower branches of a towering fir tree fall away in a dense forest. Indeed, one can already recognize in the youth the promise of sound, straight growth. The luxuriant passionateness of the southerner, with which he had become acquainted as a young man of twenty-two in the neighborhood of Nîmes (Uzès), he regarded with distrust and grave disapproval. On this subject he reported to his friend Le Vasseur: "Although I find much pleasure in chatting with you, I cannot do so for very long, because I had a visit this afternoon that took all the time I had to devote to you. My visitor was a young man of this town, very good looking, but passionately in love. I would have you know that in this country there is hardly such a thing as moderate love: all the passions here are immoderate, and the minds of this town, light enough in other things, engage their affections more strongly than in any other country in the world. . . . Well, he came to speak to me at great length on this subject, and he showed me letters, discourses, and even poems, without which they believe love-making to be impossible. I, for my part, should prefer to make love in good prose than in bad verse, but they cannot bring themselves to do that and want to be poets at any cost."[21] He concluded an account of a girl's suicide with the words: "Such is the temperament of the people of this country, and they carry their passions to the last extreme."[22] In so far as he could, be avoided contacts with these dangerous, unpredictable, quarrelsome, eccentric people, who were distasteful to him even in their exaggerated politeness. In everything he strove for the normal measure.

No tinsel, no falseness, nothing in any way contrived ever attracted this sterling connoisseur of life—nothing except the theater, and its actresses. But the latter had to be spiritual and genuine in their own way, too, if they were to captivate him. Much has been assumed but little is definitely known about his affairs with Du Parc and Champmeslé. It may be that in these he tasted the sweet poison of sensual passion to its bitterest dregs;

nevertheless here, too, there was something positive and genuine, namely, zeal for his great art and its interpretation.

As for the stage successes that he strove after so passionately and the literary fame that he fought for, it is a resounding proof of Racine's bourgeois realism that even in the days of his most brilliant triumphs and achievements he regarded these with distrust and never became intoxicated with them. The more he became aware of the unreliable transience of such victories, the more cautiously did he pursue and grasp at them—as if they were slippery eels—and the less did he respect them in his heart of hearts. Abusive criticism from an envious person could irritate and annoy him more than the unanimous applause of the masses could gratify him. This was obviously because he could not escape the feeling that artistic successes and laurels were frivolous, transient things. When an unfrivolous person once gives himself up to courting Dame Fortune's smiles, the consciousness that he is chasing a shadow makes him still more grim, irritable, and envious, until at last he gives up, sick to death of the sham. The fact that a Le Clerc, a Pradon, or a Boyer was able to awaken an audience's enthusiasm and emotion for a few hours just as well as he could, was intolerable to him, and he began to feel more and more ashamed of his colleagues, his rivals, and his calling. In the disillusionment of his maturer years he was wont to say to his son: "Do not believe that it is my plays that bring me the caresses of great persons. Corneille writes verse a hundred times more beautiful than mine, and yet no one looks at him; they love him only through of his actors. I, on the other hand, instead of wearying worldlings with recitals of my works, of which I never speak, entertain them with the things that please them. My gift in dealing with them is, not to make them feel that I am clever, but rather to teach them that they are."[23]

Hence it must have seemed to him to be a gain and a rise to more enduring things when, in 1677, he was appointed, together with Boileau, a "royal historiographer," *historiographe du Roy*. Nowadays only a few Racine experts know how very seriously he took this assignment, how much time and trouble he devoted to it, and to what extent he sacrificed his physical and domestic comfort to it for twenty-two years. True, quite a number of preliminary studies for the projected "Histoire du règne de Louis le Grand" are still extant, but the bulk of the work was destroyed in a fire in Saint-Cloud in the year 1726.

Even in terms of scholarship, these labors were not at all fortunate, for, like his colleague Boileau, Racine was far too deeply infected with the monarchist and imperialist mentality of his environment and the mental trend of his king, who appears to have been his hero as well, to rise to a critical standpoint. Boileau, aging and ailing, wrote on May 19, 1687: "Detached though I am from the things of this life, I am not yet indifferent to the glory of the King. Therefore you will give me pleasure if you kindly send me some particulars of his journey, since every step he takes is historic and he does nothing that is not worthy to be recounted, so to speak, to all ages."[24]

Racine's way of thinking was no different; if anything, he was still more the zealous and obsequious courtier, and the opinions of the two historiographers were completely in line with their office. One can understand that it was not *permissible* for them to have opinions of their own. Nevertheless it is strange that two intellects of their stamp should have been at ease in this subordination. Boileau certainly behaved with more reserve, and was not averse to being outstripped in zeal by his friend. Racine gave the highest and purest expression to the prevailing faith in kingship; yet this did not make him a mere flatterer and sycophant. His deep respect for the human personality, as for the royal person, of Louis XIV has an unmistakably genuine cordiality. Cicero's words are applicable here: *"Pietas magna in parentibus et propinquis, in patria maxima est."* All of Racine's conduct in life was imbued with this ancient Roman *pietas*. For him the concepts of fatherland, of the state, of the law, and of humanity were personified in his king; hence he felt himself impelled to honor, love, and respect him and, to emphasize with piety and songs of praise the human and natural and the majestic and royal features of this figure. Hence it sounds simple and pure from his lips when he says, in an address to the Academy: "All the words in the language, all their syllables, seem precious to us because we regard them as so many instruments with which to serve the glory of our august protector."[25] Similarly: "What a privilege it is, gentlemen, for every one of us, who have undertaken to celebrate such great things, each of us according to his different talents. In order to publish them, you will not have to discuss, with incredible labor, a tangled knot of intrigues. You will not even have to search in the office of his enemies. Their ill will, their impotence, their pain, is known to everyone. In short, you do not have to dread all those lengthy details of tedious chicanery that dry up the wit of the writer and make the majority of modern histories such boring reading.... In the history of the King all is life, movement, action. One has only to follow him, if one can, and to study him, and him alone, well. His history is a continual chain of marvelous events which he himself commences and which he himself finishes, actions which are as clear and intelligible when executed as they were impenetrable before execution. In a word, one miracle follows closely on another. One's attention is always intense, one's admiration always held. And one is struck no less by the grandeur and promptitude with which peace is concluded than by the rapidity with which conquests are made. Happy are those, Sir, who like you, are privileged to draw near that great Prince, and who, having contemplated him with the rest on those important occasions when he is carving out the destiny of the world, can then continue to contemplate him in his private capacity, and study him in the least actions of his life, where he is no less great, no less a hero, no less admirable, but full of equity, full of humanity, always calm, always master of himself, free of quirks, free of weakness and, in short, the most wise and most perfect of all men."[26]

Although Racine was anything but superstitious, one can picture him copying down for his history, with childish curiosity and awe, the horoscope that Tommaso Campanella had drawn up at the birth of Louis XIV,[27] making his collection of *Bons mots du Roi*,[28] putting special emphasis on the patience and mildness of the King as well as on his warlike attributes,[29] and feeling only scorn, pity, contempt, and incomprehension for the opponents and enemies of this divinely endowed sovereign.[30] One will not be surprised to learn, moreover, that from the end of 1683 he was a zealous and docile member of the so-called "Petite Académie," the Académie Royale des Inscriptions et Médailles, the activities of which were so often justly ridiculed. The task of these academicians was to produce inscriptions and memorial coins and medals glorifying the Sun King and also, on occasion, to compose and design allegories and scenery for court festivals. Le Tellier called them "*faiseurs de rébus et de chansonnettes.*"[31] What luck it was for Racine to be in court circles, consorting with dignitaries of the realm such as Colbert, field marshals such as Vauban and the Maréchal de Luxembourg, members of the old nobility such as the Duc Henri Jules de Bourbon, princes of the

Church such as Monseigneur de Noailles, Archbishop of Paris; undertaking literary commissions for Madame de Montespan and Madame de Maintenon; sitting in the great Académie and the Petite Académie as *Trésorier de France* and *Gentilhomme du Roy;* and actually rising to the inner circle of those surrounding the autocrat, and being permitted to accompany him to Marly! About this last he writes to Boileau in joyous excitement: "You would not believe how pleasant Marly is![32] The Court is quite different here, it seems to me, from Versailles. There are few people, and the King names all those who are to follow him here. Hence all those who are here feel very honored and consequently are in very good humor. The King himself is very free and indulgent when he is here. One might say that at Versailles he is completely immersed in business and that at Marly he is entirely free and can do as he pleases. He has done me the honor of speaking to me several times, and I have emerged from this as usual, that is to say, greatly charmed with him and in despair with myself, for I am never so dull as at those moments when I would most desire to be full of wit."[33]

Sometimes he was allowed to read aloud to the king in his expressive voice, and on these occasions he presented the newest parts from his and Boileau's history, or something else appropriate. His son Louis tells us an anecdote about it that is characteristic of both men. "The King liked to hear him read and treasured his unusual talent of letting the beauty of the work speak out. When, one day, the King was out of sorts, he bade him find a book for his diversion. My father suggested something from Plutarch's *Lives.* 'It is Gallic,' replied the King, whereupon my father bound himself to change the outmoded phraseology while reading and to set new words in the place of those fallen from use since Amyot. The King declared himself agreeable to this kind of reading, and my father, who had the honor to read aloud to him, changed everything that, through its old-fashionedness, could perhaps offend the ear of his illustrious listener, so successfully that the King listened with pleasure and apparently everyone enjoyed the beauties of Plutarch; naturally the honor that came thereby to this unofficial reader set the official ones against him."[34]

But like the greatest stage successes, the good fortune of favor at court also had its bitter side: all the more because Racine could not take it lightheartedly as an earthly enchantment, but pursued it with deep, inner gullibility. One day, at the beginning of the year 1698, he aroused—we do not know exactly how—the displeasure of the king. How deeply he felt this clouding or cooling of his master's confidence, though there is no trace of any royal reproach or punishment, one can see from his letter of March 4 to Madame de Maintenon. It ends with the words: "I assure you, Madame, that I am very worthy of the compassion which I have always seen you show for the unfortunate. I am deprived of the honor of seeing you; I hardly dare to count any longer on your protection, which is nevertheless the only protection I have sought to merit. I seek my consolation at least in my work, but you can judge the bitterness that is cast on this work by the thought that the same great prince whom I continually strive to serve may possibly regard me as a man more worthy of his anger than of his bounties."[35]

Perhaps it was a trifle, some passing mood of the sovereign, some tactlessness on the part of the poet, or some slander current at court. But Racine had a conviction, full of foreboding, that his deep regard and loving anxiety for the Christians of Port Royal must have displeased the Gallican and pro-Jesuit king.

Before his horrified eyes there now erupted, in the world around him, a conflict that, so far as we know, he had never shared in spirit or experienced with clear consciousness. He thus hastened to clear himself of any suspicion of Jansenism: "I know that, in the King's mind, a Jansenist is altogether a man of intrigue and a rebel to the Church. Be good enough to remember, Madame, how often you have said that the best quality you find in me is a childlike submission to all that the Church believes and commands, even in the smallest things. At your order I have made almost three thousand verses on religious themes; in them I have assuredly spoken from the fullness of my heart, and I have put into them all the sentiments with which I have been most deeply imbued. Has it ever come back to you that anything approaching what is called Jansenism has ever been found anywhere among these sentiments?"[36]

And just as he had remained loyal to the Church in every situation throughout his life, he had likewise remained loyal to the king: "In whatever company I have found myself, God has given me the grace never to blush either for the King or for the Gospel."

It was Racine's way and his destiny to hope and try, again

and again, by dint of his own pliability and his capacity for compromise and renunciation, to escape collision with public opinion and powers. And nothing caused him such painful surprise as to find that this course is possible only at the cost of one's character. For, once his character had become formed on reaching maturity, he could not and would not pay this price. So he now proceeded gradually to withdraw himself from court life and public life, just as he had withdrawn from the life of the theater twenty years earlier.

I do not believe that one can see either of these great renunciations as representing a sudden break. Racine was not a man of violent resolutions; it was his habit to avoid everything radical. Cautiously and gradually he altered the course of his little bark of life. The *Memoirs* of his son Louis make his principles appear more rigid, his manner of life stricter, and his decisions sharper and harsher than they probably were in reality. For instance, Louis seems to be indulging in flowery exaggeration, prompted by filial respect, when he tells of his father's turning away from drama and literature: "I now come to the happy moment when the deep piety with which my father had been imbued from childhood, and which had only been slumbering in his heart for a long while, suddenly woke to life again. Now he admitted that the authors of theatrical works are public poisoners, and he realized that he himself was perhaps one of the most dangerous of the species. He resolved not only to write no more tragedies, and indeed no more verse of any kind, but also to atone by stern penance for all he had done. So intense was his remorse that he planned to become a Carthusian monk. His confessor at the time, a God-fearing priest of his parish and a doctor of the Sorbonne, considered this solution of his problem really too violent, and pointed out that a nature such as his would not bear solitude for long, and that it would be wiser for him to remain in the world and to protect himself against its dangers by marrying a truly pious woman."[37]

Actually Racine still occupied himself with dramatic plans after this. We possess a draft in prose of an "*Iphigenia in Tauris*" which could just as well have been written after as before his *Phèdre*. He also appears to have been considering an "*Alceste.*" Even if one chooses to place these plans and experiments *before* the so-called conversion, the fact remains that three years later (1680) he allowed himself to be chosen by Madame de Montespan and her sister to compose the libretto for an opera, *La Chute de Phaéton,*[38] and in 1685 he agreed to do a musical play, *Idylle sur la Paix,* for the Marquis de Seignelay on the occasion of a wedding and peace celebration at court.[39] Worse still, he could not resist pouring scorn on some dramatic works of Fontenelle, Pradon, Longpierre, and Boyer (in the years 1681, 1694, and 1695) in very malicious epigrams. True, he did not publish these, but he did put them in circulation. And they definitely are not the only epigrams, and certainly not the worst, with which he has been credited and reproached. "Why did he have to bother with those wretched tragedies if he had renounced all literary vanities? The old man in him was dying a painfully slow death," his editor and biographer Paul Mesnard justly remarks.[40]

And is not the old man, the stage-loving singer of dark passions, just as much alive in *Athalie*—in fact, even stronger than before—as in *Andromaque* and *Bajazet?* The sharp cleavage that Racine maintained existed between his secular dramas and the Biblical plays of his later period—a cleavage recognized by many a literary historian, overaddicted to classifying—represents a demarcation that may perhaps be correct when applied to dead matter but is not true of the inspired poet. In short, in the year of his so-called conversion (1677) Racine did *not* change, but he did become quickened and strengthened when he left the boards of the theater and stepped onto the dignified and natural soil of his fatherland, assumed public offices, and started a family. And in the year that he lost the king's favor (1698) he took a further and final step toward permanent stability by curtailing his attendance at court and living as much as possible with his family. After this he appeared at Versailles and Marly only for the sake of his children's future. On July 24, 1698, he wrote to his eldest son: "As soon as the time comes to propose something for you... you may be sure that I shall not neglect those opportunities when they come, no longer having anything that keeps me at Court except the thought of placing you in the position of no longer having need of me.... I certainly feel that the time is coming when I must give some thought to retiring."[41]

The assertion of that malicious collector of court gossip, the Duc de Saint-Simon, that Racine died of grief over his loss of the king's favor, can only find credence among those who have no inkling of what a joyous, happy, and normal husband and father our poet was, and how calm and deeply rooted was his faith. He died of a cancer of the liver, not of thwarted ambition.

To assess properly the sterling gold of his heart, its tenderness, purity, and wisdom, we must see him in the bosom of his family. The charm and grace, devoid of all artificiality and sentimentality, of his dealings with children and young people, is part of his native genius as an artist. His son Louis tells his grandson Jean of this: "The man whose name you have been told so often, indeed too often, that you must renew, was never so happy as when, free from the duties of the Court that he had so enjoyed in earlier years, he could come home to us for a few days. He had the courage to play his role as father even in the presence of strange guests. He joined in all our games, and I remember that in our processions—I know I can write this to you—in which my sisters played the other clergy and I the parish priest, the author of *Athalie* used to carry the cross at our head and join in our hymns."[42]

He took children seriously, and even in their games and fun tried constantly to edify them, or to help them along with kindly teasing. One can see from his letters[43] how he watched over the studies, reading, and even purity of speech of his eldest son, Jean Baptiste. But above all he tried to save his seven children from the dangers, disappointments, and conflicts that he knew and feared. One gets the impression that his whole method of education was based on prudence and realism, and that he was more concerned to supervise his children's paths in life than to develop their personalities and aptitudes. To be sure, their natural *joie de vivre* and youthful gaiety could only assert itself occasionally and exceptionally under his fatherly guidance. Racine kept his home not exactly joyless, but certainly not overflowing with joyousness. He felt half edified and half dismayed when his daughters, one after another, expressed their desire to flee the world and take the veil. "Ultimately he blamed himself in part for this. The good upbringing he had given the girl[44] and the devout spirit with which he had imbued her, led her to the altar of this sacrifice; she believed what he had told her," wrote Père Quesnel[45] on one such occasion. His anxious love for his wife and children and his solicitude for their welfare made his domestic life a bittersweet burden that often proved almost too heavy for him. For the aim he had set himself was a dual one that was not in fact easy to combine: to further with equal zeal the spiritual and the material well-being of his family. When racked with domestic cares—the illness of his children, for instance—he used often to lament, his son Louis tell us, "Why have I exposed myself to this? Why was I persuaded not to become a Carthusian? I would have had much more peace."[46]

Often, when one sees how he took any and every occasion to urge caution and discretion on his relatives, his friends, and the Jansenists, one feels that he lacked courage for life and that his was a nature without ardor, that he handled matters of the heart, such as the marriages of his children, and even his own marriage, as business transactions. Such matters were in fact business matters to him, not commercial transactions but transactions of moral duty and responsibility.[47] Accordingly as this feeling and sense of responsibility became clearer in him, he turned away ever more resolutely from everything false and transitory and toward what alone is enduring and strong—toward God. He worked increasingly toward this final goal, driven on by disappointment after disappointment, renunciation after renunciation; and as he progressed thus, he tended to feel his wordly involvement growing more irksome and life becoming more difficult. When he knew the end was near, he showed no inclination to retrace his way a single step. The doctors tried to deceive him with hopes, but he said to his son: "They will say what they like; let them say it; but you, my son, would you, too, wish to deceive me, and to conspire with them in doing so? God is master; but I can assure you that if He were to give me the choice of life or death, I do not know which I would choose; the price has been paid."[48]

2

The Man and His Time

Racine did not conform in any way—in his character, his manner of life, or even his works—to the popular image of the poet as current today. For he was neither dreamy nor aloof from the world, neither impractical and easy-going like La Fontaine nor inflexible and "awkward" like Corneille, nor misanthropic and somberly heroic in outlook like Molière. Neither was he harrowed and world weary like the Romantic poets nor, like Dante and Goethe, of stern or gay superiority of intellect. He was not even passionate and resigned to fate as were his beloved exemplars, the Greek tragic poets.

A strange absence of the play of the imagination distinguishes him from even the kindlier and more harmonious poets, Virgil, Ariosto, and Cervantes, who are relatively nearer to him in spirit. None of the great ones of Parnassus ever made himself at home among the prosaic things of daily life as completely as he; none has ever been so deeply imbued with the ideas that dominated his time. Hence he must be regarded, not only in the historical and psychological sense but also in his directly active mental disposition, as a child of secularism. None of the great poets has thought and written so little of a symbolical or mythical nature; none has thought and written so soberly and simply—or succeeded in being to such a great extent a poet of the unpoetical. In other words, none has equaled him in finding pure and authentic poetry where the ordinary person only perceives the ordinary and the banal. Racine's particular genius, it seems to me, lay in his exceptional capacity for ennobling material life—the earthy, unimaginative activities of men, their habits colored by the fashion of the time, their natural instincts and feelings, in short, all their inveterate vulgarity. It was given him to breathe the air of this commonness without hatred, indignation, or disgust, and not to become lost in it; to see through it completely and to find and tread, through this labyrinth, the way to purity—the way of silent renunciation.

If I were to reduce Racine to a formula, I would call him, not the singer of the passions, particularly of the sexual passions, as most of his interpreters do, but rather the poet of renunciation.

Renunciation? In what sense, of what, and for love of whom? One could say, in sum, renunciation of all things temporal for the sake of the eternal. But Racine is new and unique precisely because the renunciation he means and proclaims is no penitential, monkish, or medieval denial, no abrupt turning away from the world, no break with it on grounds of principle. On the contrary, he strives, slowly and painfully, occasion by occasion, to extricate himself from its toils. In his efforts to rise toward the heights, he has no wings or other magic means, but walks on a pair of honest human feet. Only by this simple means does renunciation ennoble the dust on which it walks.

If we would understand Racine completely, we must know the vital interests of his countrymen and his time, the interests among which he lived and above which he rose. Precisely because he himself never argued out these matters critically with himself, precisely because he never arrogated to himself either a philosophical or a prophetic position, one has to work out the line of his world view and the instinctive trend of his intellect.

His intellectual career ran its course in the time of the Counter Reformation or, one might say, in the period of transition from the Renaissance to the Enlightenment and the Romantic period. The French part in the Counter Reformation consisted in striving for the consolidation and unification of the authority of state and Church while at the same time fighting and weakening the European power that stood in the forefront of this same effort, namely, Spain. Hence, while France was suppressing Protestantism, the trend toward the formation of small autonomous states, and individualism of every kind within her own realm, she was zealously aiding and abetting these same trends abroad. The thought more or less consciously underlying this double game was that there is no rigid antithesis between the principle of authority and the principle of freedom, but rather a mobile reciprocity that must be regulated and exploited. This insight, which was less familiar to the inflexible thought and political science of the Spaniards, gave the French of the seventeenth century an unbiased liveliness and agility of mind which won them pre-eminence over all other nations. Their superiority during that period rested on the sureness and quickness of their sense of what suited a given time or situation. Politically they were the most gifted race. We have seen already how much of this national genius Racine had absorbed, and how ingrained in him was the political and diplomatic sense of tact that dominated his whole way of life.

One can understand that the danger of a loss of principles through practicing this adroit opportunism was very great, particularly after the wars of religion had shown the terrors and horrors to which inflexibility can lead. Hence, after its bloody victories, the Catholic Church turned as naturally and adroitly as possible back to its spiritual mission, to good works, and to the peaceful recovery of its renegade and disaffected members, and sought to make contact with the world in a new way.

It was above all Saint Francis de Sales (1567–1622) who made Catholic piety not only practical, which it had always been, but also social, approachable, genial, friendly, amiable, and dexterous. He lent it the grace and elegance that Huguenot piety lacked. "It is an error and hence a heresy to wish to banish the devout life from the company of soldiers, the workshop of artisans, the court of princes, the household of the married," he wrote to his spiritual friend, Madame de Charmoisy, in his *Introduction à la vie dévote*. "It has even happened that some have lost perfection in that solitude which nevertheless is so desirable for perfection, and have preserved it among the multitude, which seems so unfavorable to perfection, Games, balls, feasts, pomps, plays, are in no way bad in themselves, but merely indifferent, for one can use them either well or badly; nevertheless all these things are dangerous, and to delight in them is still more dangerous. I say, then, Philothée, that even if it be lawful to play, dance, dress up in finery, listen to moral plays, and feast at banquets, if one delights in all that, it is a thing contrary to devotion and extremely harmful and dangerous. It is not bad to do it, but it is bad to find one's delight in it."[1]

The great thing was to be present everywhere in the world,

to take part in everything, to make oneself useful, influential, powerful, pleasant, and amiable in it, and yet not to fall for it. Hence the necessity for the person living in the world, whether king, court lady, or bourgeois, to be kept on a spiritual director's leash and to be guided by him, as occasion arose, in all temptations, perplexities, doubts, and scruples of conscience. Hence too the importance of the confessional, of moral theology and casuistry, of Christian yet worldly, pious yet social, rules of life, and the increasing influence of the Society of Jesus, which was the most adroit and flexible teacher and guide in all these things.[2]

This kind of Christianity, this Counter Reformation piety, which aimed at belonging wholly to heaven inwardly and wholly to the world outwardly,[3] and therefore had to distrust itself, watch itself, and master itself always, favored the cultivation of those contrived, broken, theatrical, illusionistic, rhetorical, and—for all their liveliness—static art forms[4] which today we call Baroque, and which are characterized by the aim of external effect and internal restraint. In France they are to be found in all tones—Italianate, Spanish style, sweet, precious, solemn, and Roman, academical, jocose, burlesque, Arcadian, chivalric, adventurous, heroic, sentimental, bourgeois, witty, ornate, of studied carelessness, stoical, cynical, Epicurean, gallant, and so on. This spectacular period style, for which all visible phenomena are only illusory and all nature is only contrivance, had captivated Racine in the beginning, but he had subsequently overcome its fascination.

Just as he had found his way, as a moral being, back to authenticity and wholeness from division between God and the world, so too, as a poet, with still firmer determination and greater success, he had renounced all the illusion and artificiality of the Baroque. The link that connects his character as artist and his way of life is the impulse toward inward and outward simplicity and authenticity.[5]

In this aim he had found zealous help in Jansenism.

Not only the Jesuits but also the Jansenists had points of contact with Saint Francis de Sales. In pastoral work, especially, they had learned from him, and even from the Spanish mystics. From the latter they had learned many practical principles of monastic reform.[6] For in this particular they were wholly Catholic, orthodox, and anything but Protestant-minded: they regarded the docile submissiveness of the laity as necessary and the spiritual authority of the priest as unconditional. Indeed, they lapsed into the medieval type of monasticism, exceeded themselves in penances of the crudest kind, fasted to excess, performed the lowliest manual labour between their theological and philosophical studies, and some of them even regarded it as particularly virtuous to renounce personal cleanliness.

But their importance is to be sought less in this violent renunciation of the things of the senses than in their practice of the contemplative life. Their teaching on grace is the expression of their feeling of the direct and personal relation of the individual to his God. There is no need to enter into detail here concerning their theological arguments and quarrels with the Jesuits, the Sorbonne, and Rome.[7] But it is definitely necessary to make clear the fundamental position from which they started and in which they are still caught up, right to the present day. Humble acceptance and recognition of the authoritative, grace-giving character of the Church, the priestly office, and the sacraments, on the one hand, and the self-sufficient Protestant spirituality and subjectivity in regard to the doctrine of salvation on the other hand—ecclesiastical obedience and religious primitiveness—how could these dwell together in the same breast? After the Council of Trent, after the excommunication and condemnation as heretics of Luther and Calvin, was there still an honorable possibility of entertaining these opposite concepts within the Roman Church? Could purity of conscience be compatible with tutelage of conscience? This is the simplest statement of the problem that tortured the Jansenists within and without, politically and ethically. Their essentially evangelical, Pauline, Augustinian, anti-Pelagian, reformatory piety tried to claim not only the right of a home but actually the right of domination within the old Church. This was an anachronism as naïve as it was romantic, and comparable, in terms of the State, with the unsuccessful rebellion known as the *Fronde*, whose leader, Paul de Gondi, Cardinal de Retz, had in fact Jansenist leanings, or at least flirted and went part of the way with the Port-Royal people.

Viewed from the human side, however, the Jansenist movement is one of those age-old, touching efforts to preserve purity of heart in the midst of daily material existence, and purity of ideals in a world of compromise. For the most deeply cherished doctrine of the Jansenists, the idea of predestination, is not merely something Christian, it is something human. It is proper to all deep piety. Even the Greeks, with their myths of Hercules, Theseus, Hippolytus, Phedra, Agamemnon, Iphigenia, Cassandra, and Andromache as favorites or victims of their gods, were deeply imbued with it. A purely just deity, a god whose justice is correct and calculable, is no living god but a mere concept.

That the core of the Jansenist faith was very much Racine's, too, is clear from the fact that it did not move and impel him merely as a theological controversy, nor solely—as it did the great Pascal—as a question of Christian faith, but that, on the contrary, he felt it, experienced it, and gave it form in the secular, even in the pagan sphere, in fantasy, in yearning and ardor, in "profane" literature, and that the Greek tragic dramatists Euripides and Sophocles had their place as his decisive exemplars alongside Antoine Arnauld and the other men and women of Port-Royal.

Hence his connection with Jansenism was a curiously semi-obscure dual relationship, the ambiguity of which must have inevitably oppressed him. But now that the circumstances can be seen clearly and assessed rightly, this ambiguity should no longer be interpreted as lack of character on his part. If he ever doubted any Jansenist tenet in his secret heart, it can never have been the doctrine of predestination, but it may possibly have been original sin and the sinfulness of the world. Religious determinism lay deep in his soul and was the very breath of his spirit. He found his highest bliss in the thought that God upheld and permeated the universe with His power and His love, and established it in His peace:

> Le jour annonce au jour sa gloire et sa puissance,
> Tout l'univers est plein de sa magnificence.
> . . . .
> Il donne aux fleurs leur admirable peinture.
> Il fait naître et mûrir les fruits.
> Il leur dispense avec mesure
> Et la chaleur des jours et la fraîcheur des nuits;
> Le champ qui les reçut les rend avec usure,
> Il commande au soleil d'animer la nature,
> Et la lumière est un don de ses mains;
> Mais sa loi sainte, sa loi pure
> Est le plus riche don qu'il ait fait aux humains.[8]

> Day tells day of his glory and power, the entire universe is fraught with his magnificence.
>
> ....
>
> He gives the flowers their wonderful colors. He makes the fruits grow and ripen. He carefully supplies them with the warmth of day and the coolness of night, which the fields receive and return with interest, he commands the sun to animate nature, and light is a gift from his hands; but his holy law, his pure law, is his richest gift to man.

On the other hand, the thing that he found hard to believe and that became a certainty for him only by bitter experience and his own sinfulness, was the existence of evil.

> Moi! je pourrois trahir le Dieu que j'aime?[9]

> I! Could I betray the God I love?

Doubtless a person like him could only go astray through guileless youthful high spirits or childishly careless pliancy, in other words, through frivolity. Hence the Jansenist's penitential spirit and flight from the world inevitably impressed him at first as petty timidity, antediluvian stuffiness. It was as such that he mocked it in his *Lettre à l'auteur des Imaginaires*.

But at about the same time—in fact, two years earlier (1664)—he had lashed out in epigrammatic verse against all those who, for the sake of peace with the Church, departed one iota from the Jansenist teaching on grace and signed the notorious *Formulaire*.

> Contre Jansénius j'ai la plume à la main,
> Je suis prêt à signer tout ce qu'on me demande.
> Qu'il soit hérétique ou romain,
> Je veux conserver ma prébende.[10]

> I take up my pen against Jansenius, I am ready to sign whatever I am asked to. Whether he be heretic or Roman, I want to safeguard my prebend.

Hence we see that in the days of his deepest worldly involvement he regarded the Jansenists as at once right and wrong—

right in their teaching on grace, wrong in their teaching on sin, penance, denial of the world and scorn for the arts.

But the sweet core and the hard outer shell of this piety were so deeply intergrown that he could only have kept up his dual attitude toward Jansenism at the price of inner ambiguity and division of heart. Among his *Cantiques spirituels* of the year 1694 there is a piece which is frequently cited as a confession of this division of heart:

Mon Dieu, quelle guerre cruelle!
Je trouve deux hommes en moi:
L'un veut que plein d'amour pour toi
Mon cœur te soit toujours fidèle.
L'autre à tes volontés rebelle
Me révolte contre ta loi.

L'un tout esprit, et tout céleste,
Veut qu'au ciel sans cesse attaché,
Et des biens éternels touché,
Je compte pour rien tout le reste;
Et l'autre par son poids funeste
Me tient vers la terre penché.

Hélas! En guerre avec moi-même,
Où pourrai-je trouver la paix?
Je veux, et n'accomplis jamais.
Je veux, mais, ô misère extrême!
Je ne fais pas le bien que j'aime,
Et je fais le mal que je hais.

O grâce, ô rayon salutaire,
Viens me mettre avec moi d'accord;
Et domptant par un doux effort
Cet homme qui t'est si contraire,
Fais ton esclave volontaire
De cet esclave de la mort.[11]

My God, what a cruel war! There are two men in me: the one wants my heart—full of love for you—to remain faithful to you always. The other—rebelling against your commands—turns me against your law.

> The one, all spirit, all celestial, wants me ever attached to heaven and moved by the everlasting, counting the rest for naught; and the other, by its deadly weight, keeps me bent toward earth.
>
> Alas! At war with myself, where could I find peace? I wish, and never achieve, I wish, but O extreme wretchedness, I do not do the good I love, and I do the evil that I abhor.
>
> O grace, O salutary beam, come set me at peace with myself; and by a gentle effort conquering this man so rebellious to you, make into your willing slave, this slave of death.

Confessional poetry, in the modern sense of the word, was something that neither Racine nor any other poet of his period permitted himself. For to them moral and religious teachings were as clear and firm as crystal—matters of general validity that *could* not become undefined, vague, or problematical for the individual. Hence this *cantique* did not stem from direct spiritual anguish on the part of the poet, but rather from a devout recollection of some texts in Saint Paul's Epistle to the Romans (VII, 18–25), and must be regarded not as a personal outburst but as a sensitive translation and expression of a typically Christian state of mind, in which each of us was to see and recognize himself, as Louis XIV actually did. On hearing the first verses sung, the king is said to have whispered to Madame de Maintenon: "Madame, here are two men that I know well!"

Racine was no split personality, no torn being. That is to say, he was so only about as much or as little as any of us when we fall from our ideals or try to deny nature too severely. He never considered his conflict between temporal and eternal things to be either admirable or praiseworthy; this division was in fact only delay and hesitation on his upward course, not a real estrangement of heart. Moreover, there is no evidence that in his more mature years he had ever again criticized the flight from the world or the penitential spirit of his Jansenist teachers and friends. True, he often exhorted them to discretion, but never counseled tepidity in their arguments with secular and ecclesiastical authorities. To be sure, he would have preferred to see them spared conflict and martyrdom. But as their plight became more acute he felt morally bound to take sides with them, and so he began to write down the history of this painful struggle.

The internal and external motives and occasions that provoked his famous *Abrégé de l'histoire de Port-Royal* are almost impossible to unravel or elucidate today. We cannot know whether it was meant for a prince of the Church, or for secular potentates, or only for a circle of friends, or—as seems to me the most likely—for a more distant and less inimical future age. Racine worked on it up to his death and handed over the unfinished manuscript, which he had been hiding from his family as something potentially incriminating, to a friend of like mind, probably the doctor, Denis Dodart, for safekeeping. As long as the Jesuits' partisans were in power in France, publication could not be thought of. The first part of the *Abrégé* was published in Cologne in 1742, and the second—unfinished—part in 1767.

With this history of the Abbey of Port-Royal, Racine not only repaid a debt of thanks to the guardians and benefactors of his youth but also made the cause of Port-Royal his own, and now not merely in a literary, nostalgic, lyrical, or fanciful way, but with firm and sober knowledge and deliberation, in simple prose.

His will, dated October 10, 1698, begins: "I desire that after my death my body be carried to Port-Royal des Champs, and that it be buried in the cemetery, at the foot of the grave of M. Hamon"[12]

A wag is said to have commented on this: "He would never have done that while he was alive!"[13] In actual fact, while he "was still alive" Racine laid his spiritual nature to rest in Port-Royal. It is precisely for this reason that his *Histoire* of this abbey is an interment rather than an argument, an apologia rather than a criticism. If anyone still reads it today, it is not in order to learn of the importance of Port-Royal in the history of the Church and of the faith, nor even to become acquainted with Racine's own relation to Jansenism. For this relation, as one can see at once, is that of an advocate toward his protegé. In the main, this work is still read only for the sake of the perfect prose in which it is written. Gustave Lanson regards it as "*the* masterpiece of historical literature of the seventeenth century."

Its value and charm lie, in fact, in the form, and this means more than perfect diction. The beauty of expression here is nothing less than the clear reflection of a purified spirit looking back with love and religious devotion on the struggles of man's imperishable conscience against temporal powers. Even the most exciting conflict is described with perfect equanimity, for it is tacitly assumed that all the suffering, all the defenselessness, all the heroism of soul and all the spiritual joy, in short, all the higher righteousness, is on the side of Port-Royal, and that all the power, blindness of heart, and malice is on the side of Port-Royal's enemies.

To the critical historical thought of today it must seem highly debatable, in fact impossible, that might and right should be as naturally incompatible and inconsistent as oil and water. If that were the case, all the hidden ferment, the tensions, the dynamism, and the dialectic would be eliminated from historical narratives. Viewed in the light of this philosophy of history, one may indeed say that Racine's history of Port-Royal is a dreary and tedious book. But in order to understand its peculiar charm, one must regard it as a legend, even if it is a legend worked out unusually conscientiously and soberly in its way, but limited by its author's unshakable faith in the holiness of Port-Royal and definitely written with an apologetic intent.

In short, if I am not entirely mistaken, Racine intended and undertook this *Abrégé* as an account of the wonders and sufferings of the house of Port-Royal for the purpose of defending it and reestablishing it in public esteem. The real hero of the whole narrative—and this lends the pious legend a modern, journalistic, and in fact almost philosophical touch—is not this or that person, but the house, the monastery, the institution, the party of Port-Royal, with its spirit and its faith. Similarly, the enemies are not flesh and blood villains, but parties, institutions, offices, organizations—impersonal, intellectual forces: the Sorbonne, the Jesuit order, the episcopate, the monarchy with its representatives, and so on. The truly modern expertise in this narrative art, so reminiscent of the legend and the fairy tale, consists in the way the human, the all too human, on the one hand and the divine guidance on the other hand are scented out, as it were, from behind these suprapersonal forces, and the ideological nature of the great conflict emerges from a wealth of small and petty incidents, squabbles, intrigues, and misunderstandings, of which the repercussions are reflected, again.

in personal quarrels and gossip. Hence the reader finds himself alternately edified and scandalized, overwhelmed with devout respect at one moment and smiling ironically and indulgently the next. But all the time, behind the lucid narrative, we admire the noble and exalted nature of the man who, despite all his universality of vision and his brilliance, had proved capable of silently rejecting this cruel, strange world and all its ways, and this without either hatred or passion—even without regret.

To be sure, he only half succeeds in making the events of his *Histoire* really live. True, he uncovers their highly complicated interrelations industriously and ingeniously. But how could the dogmatic core of the conflict—namely, the doctrine of grace—ever have become a problem to him, the devout believer, blessed with grace? He relates the "Miracle of the Holy Thorn," for instance, without batting an eyelid, as if it were something absolutely beyond question. And, on the other hand, why should he still be particularly shaken, in his Christian detachment of heart, by the character and behavior of Port-Royal's opponents? In former days he had never spoken so quietly and dispassionately of his king as he does here: "I have no doubt that posterity, seeing one day, on the one hand the great things that the King has done for the advancement of the Catholic religion, and on the other hand the great services that M. Arnauld has rendered to the Church, and the extraordinary virtue that has shone forth in the house of which we speak, will find it hard to understand how it could have happened that, under the reign of a king so full of peity and justice, such a holy house should have been destroyed and that the same M. Arnauld should have been obliged to go and end his days in foreign countries. But this is not the first time that God has permitted truly great saints to be treated as evildoers by truly virtuous princes. The Church's history is full of similar examples; and it must be acknowledged that never has prejudice been based on reasons more apparent than this prejudice of the King against everything known as Jansenism.

To be sure, Racine is dropping a small grain of incense here too. But it is the last one. A cold, otherworldly air, at times tiresome for the reader, pervades the presentation of events and of people that, after all, were once so deeply and painfully close to the narrator's heart. He now takes leave of them.

3

Racine's Works

Their Special Nature

In spite of their simplicity and clarity, Racine's works are even more difficult for today's readers to understand than are the life and character of their curiously reserved creator. A form as simple, restrained, and temperate as he created is likely to be misunderstood, disregarded, or totally unrecognized by our contemporary taste. For Romanticism, naturalism, and expressionism have gradually inured us to increasingly intemperate forms of expression. And it is not only the formal appearance, not only the style, of Racine's writings that seems to lack color beside the styles of other periods. Their content, too, their whole temper, is strangely out of tune with a time like the present, so dominated by action and external effect. Hence to advocate Racine is a pretty hopeless business wherever one looks in our present-day world. We must be content if we succeed in refuting at least the most common prejudices that stand in the way even of those with the best will to understand his art.[1]

Undoubtedly the greatest obstacle between ourselves and Racine is the French language. For his verse does not translate well, as repeated experience tells us. The best thing in Racine—the direct effect on the mind through the ear—is lost in translation. We fail, in the first place, in the transitions from dialogue to song that mark the whole of Racine's tragic drama. Our recitative is too reminiscent of opera or melodrama; and the style in which we are used to hearing the blank verse of our dramatists declaimed could adapt itself fairly well to Corneille's or Voltaire's verse drama, but is decidedly too accentuated, too dynamic, too bombastic for Racine. And where voice and ear do not act in concert, there is no public for Racine.

Moreover, as metrical and rhythmic form, Racine's alexandrines seem to us slow and difficult, and almost defy imitation in our language. His harmony strikes us as monotonous, his biarticulation pedantic, his rhyme obtrusive, until we have learned to sense in this apparently rigid form the living emotion, the flexibility, the unobtrusive inner freedom, and the pulsating succession of feelings.

In order to gain a perception of Racine's qualities, which are too delicate to be grasped in concepts, I know of no better practice than to become familiar with them through the senses; to exercise the ear tirelessly on his language, to let his verses work on us again and again, to learn them by heart until they become natural to us and whisper to our souls. And then our spirit will yield to them of itself.

Admittedly, once we have at last acquired the ability to absorb the directly lyrical elements of Racine's drama, we experience a second disappointment. For we find that we have *not* got hold of *him*, or of his emotional world, or even of his attitude of mind or convictions. He does not reveal himself in aphorisms, sayings, or personal outbursts. He does not lend himself well to quotation. True, some magnificent word pictures—but no really winged words—stand out from the austere texture of his dramas. He evades us and disappears behind the solid restraint of the work. Our modern taste for the aphoristic and fragmentary, our impatient addiction to anthologies, can expect little or nothing from him. Even his individual characters lack sufficient definition to make it viable to lift them out of their environment and their situation, and to treat them as independent monuments, symbols, or types, such as Hamlet, Faust, or Molière's misanthrope.

There is a widely shared view, based above all on Shakespeare's works, that the highest duty and achievement of the poet consists in creating human characters that are self-sufficient, stand on their own feet, have their own mental attitudes, frames of mind, views, modes of expression, physiognomies, and in maintaining, unfolding, and developing these or, alternatively, letting them perish. Those who hold this view will find that it does not apply to Racine. They must leave that particular yardstick—the man of letters as creator of human beings—at home when they enter Racine's theater.

On the other hand, it is all the more necessary to bring to Racine a feeling and understanding for social life, for the forms of social communication, for surprising and delicate situations, for customs, rules of etiquette, the art of tactfulness, human aberrations, embarrassments, the arts of polite living, for indiscretions, and the like. But the basic prerequisite is a sense for the pulsebeat of humanity in general and of French society in the seventeenth century in particular.

On Molière's and Racine's stage, as Gundolf remarked on the occasion of the first production of Kleist's *Amphitryon*, "the pure ego had no autonomy; it was only a member of the living, decisive law called society.... The self had to put up with this, to come to terms with one way or another—by society it was only assessed as comic or tragic; it had no law and no value of its own; it was the opponent or victim or plaything of society, just as the ancients were the victims or playthings of the gods or of fate. In Molière's and Racine's drama, society is what the world of myth, the gods, and fate were in the dramas of Sophocles and Aristophanes, namely, the ultimate determining force, the all-embracing horizon, against which all the individual's vital forces and all the powers of his soul stood out in contrast."[2]

We, on the other hand, tend to regard society as an unpleasantly artificial and positively unnatural restriction of the individual's nature. It seems to us to be a thing of convention and hypocrisy. Nevertheless, it is a part of reality, and like everything real, has its poetry, its exalted, dignified, charming, or comical intonation, as the case may be. It is our fault, not Racine's, if, for instance, the words the Emperor Titus addresses to Berenice,

> N'en doutez point, Madame, et j'atteste les Dieux
> Que toujours Bérénice est présente à mes yeux

> Doubt it not, Madame, and the gods are my witness, that Berenice is always before my eyes,

sound false rather than solemn and heartfelt, to our ears.

If we do not, for the sake of Racine, forget our feeling for the language of daily life and learn a new one, namely, Racine's language, we shall misinterpret him again and again, and take umbrage, like schoolchildren, at his strange mastery. If he were more distant from us and stranger than he actually is, this would come more easily to us. But our prejuidce against the whole noble, courtly system, which dates from our European past, is still in our blood today. Trifling matters in themselves, these courtly forms of address, and yet they become a stumbling block because they are associated with something greater, namely, Racine's concept of society as a supratemporal reality.

One must not hold this against him as a lack of historical sense or an anachronism, for it is based on faith—his faith in the eternally enduring bonds between human hearts. Racine regards family ties and, even more, sexual love as sacred primeval forces of human nature that lend to society and the state an elemental consecration, a nobility and a grandeur, a solemn yet heartfelt ceremonial which, though one must realistically recognize in it certain definite features of French court ceremonial, is potentially—that is to say, in the desire and imagination of the poet—valid for all countries, races, and ages. By this faith of the poet the conventional and the time-bound are fused and interwoven with the elemental and the natural. To anyone inclined to regard this as inferior or contrived and to deride, for instance, the gallantries of Racine's Alexander, Mithridates, Titus, or Achilles, one might reply with Mörike's witty couplet:

> So ist die Lieb', und war auch so,
> Wie lang es Liebe gibt,
> Und anders war Herr Salomo,
> Der Weise, nicht verliebt.

> This is love's working, this is its nature,
> Since however long there has been love.
> And Salomon the Wise
> Loved in no different way.

Moreover, the idea that the love life of the ancients was lacking in gallantry—and that primitive peoples' love life still is—must be repudiated as a crudely and naïvely materialistic belief.

Actually, it is generally the critics of the materialistic, liberal, and positivist schools who have reproached Racine with gallant eroticism—or erotic gallantry—and have actually advocated, as an antidote, a drama completely free of sexual love and of femininity. For a while such criticism may have been justified when applied to the far too numerous imitators of Racine. But as for the master himself, those who see sexual love as the focal point of his poetical inspiration misunderstand him completely. For this is true of him only in that he considers sexual love the greatest and most universal temptation, the most alluring entanglement in which men can become involved. For this reason he feels it to be tragic. But for this reason, too, another, a higher and stronger instinct, one that aspires to rise above these depths and these fateful destinies, is at work throughout his dramas. It is not that he preaches the conquest of passion as a moral requirement; to do so would be to make it a subject of rhetoric. Oh the contrary, he knows and feels and respects it as a metaphysical necessity through which his heroes go to ruin or to which they must submit. In Racine's poetical world sexual love is merely part of the natural destiny of man, but renunciation and self-conquest are his spiritual destiny. He has worked out this point of view with progressively greater clarity in all his tragedies of love from *Les Thébaïdes* to *Phèdre.* It is not difficult to trace the increasing spiritualization of his work from drama to drama. In the two last, and purest, compositions, *Esther* and *Athalie,* the erotic and gallant element finally drops into the background, leaving the whole stage free for the *religious ideal* of renunciation and sacrifice.

But with Racine fate and destiny reign everywhere, in the lovers' chamber as in the temple of sacrifice. And this fact has brought him the ultimate and most serious reproach, namely, that his art is depressing rather than inspiring. Corneille has been called the poet of free will and moral self-determination, as though Racine's characters did not possess and act with their own greatness and their own particular kind of heroism. Only they cannot reasonably do this by behaving as representatives and exemplars of an ideal principle. They do not act according to self-chosen and self-made principles and formulas like Corneille's stage heroes; hence it must be admitted that they are not ethical personalities. They play, strictly speaking, only the role that nature and God appear to have cast them for. The nobility, the propriety, the greatness, the grace, and the dignity that they are free to evince, in short, the task that is theirs, is to play their roles authentically and completely to the end, as in Calderón's drama *The Great Theater of the World.* An inner authenticity and emotion that come to light, that will show themselves, and be bodied forth and made real, from the disposition to the outward attitude, from the ethical to the aesthetic law of style: to play what one is and to be or become what one has to play—that is the morality and the superb poetic fire of Racine's heroic characters. A stage morality, if you like, not a simple everyday morality for life, and definitely no sober bourgeois virtue.

Hence it would seem that even in this very genuineness there is pose; in this authenticity there is theater. And a reproach which we glimpsed at the beginning and at least partially forestalled, arises once more with increased emphasis. Racine's art, it is said, is mere rhetorical show of feeling, not genuine spiritual poetry or vigorous racy drama. "Pseudo classicism" is the phrase sometimes used to describe it. To be sure, the advice we gave earlier—to immerse oneself in the beauties of the language and the verse, the expressive gestures, and to impress these on the mind through the ear and the eye—only means saving the external side of this art. To say, in effect, "*Ponete mente almen com' io son bella!*" seems actually to admit the superficiality of it all. If the people of Racine's dramas were in fact only players of roles, and only represent the personality without in some way *being* it, then everything they do and mean would indeed remain in the domain of illusion and effect.

On closer examination, however, it emerges that Racine's characters always have two sides and hence must always have a dual public, so to speak: the frequenter of the theater, eager to see and hear, to whom they appear merely as players of parts; and a judge of souls, who looks into the inmost heart. This second forum is the reflection, the mirroring by which these players of roles are continually surrounded, illumined, accompanied, dissected, tortured, agonized, and forced to confession, self-knowledge, and the most painful inwardness.

Literary historians are wont to call this second element psychological analysis. But considered in the light of the history of the theater, it is something quite different and essentially more tangible. It is God Himself, before Whose altar the liturgical drama was produced in the churches of medieval times. For the Easter and Christmas plays of those days were performed just as much to the glory of God, in God's presence, in the house of God, as for the edification, exhortation, instruction, entertainment, and amusement of His people. Those medieval dramas had God before them and the earthly spectators behind them. When they subsequently turned more and more toward the latter and left the house of God, they still could not rid themselves of the presence of God or lose their former attitude toward Him, even though it was now focused on the earthly. In these days we cannot trace in detail this connection, this persistence of the Christian thought of God through the theater of the later Middle Ages, the Renaissance, the Baroque period, and the neoclassical period. In Racine's dramas, at any rate, this inherited thought is omnipresent and appears in a variety of guises. But above all it penetrates the hero and causes his duality and division of heart.

In this state the hero always behaves both actively and reflectively at the same time: he witnesses his own actions as if he had a second self. At all the decisive points of a classical French drama one could transpose the words of the hero from the first person into the second or third, to such a degree do these people dissect, reflect upon, excoriate, and rise above themselves. One often has the sensation of listening to an old opera in which the same outburst of emotion is inflected and sung in all the persons, singular and plural, by two, three, or six voices at once. The famous monologues in *Titus* (IV, 4) and *Mithridate* (IV, 5) sound as though all the walls were equipped with ears and eyes, loudspeakers and mirrors, in order to bring out the very depths of the tortured human soul and make known the most secret things in it. But the monologue is not necessary for this, for even amidst tumultuous action and wordy strife the inwardness of the Racinian character hardly ever deserts him. He keeps trying to get clear about himself, and, locked into the prison cell and law court of this pitiless stage with its three dimensions, he has to be alternately his own advocate, interpreter, apologist, prosecutor, and examining judge. And because he is so inward and so thoughtful, he generally needs, in addition to the public and the partner in dialogue, his special confidant, a second self, so to speak, to the father confessor that he is already to himself.

A necessary consequence of the introspectiveness and spirituality of the humanity so exposed to view is that there is no place beside it for louts, clowns, fools, or children. As all experts on Racine have agreed, it was quite adventurous of the dramatist to introduce little Joas. His justification was that this child represents a pure and as yet undimmed consciousness of God. Athalie herself has to say:

> Cet âge est innocent. Son ingénuité
> N'altère point encor la simple vérité.
> Laissez-le s'expliquer sur tout ce qui le touche.... (II, 7)

> This age is innocent. Its artlessness has not yet altered the simple truth. Let him explain all these matters that involve him....

Racine portrays man as Godlike by virtue of his spiritual nature and inward eye, and human, all too human, in his theatrical superficiality. This dual being finds his unity precisely in the fact that people who are not blind, but perceptive and critical, wish to be watchful of themselves as they speak and act; they must not be ordinary little trivial people, but must move in high circles, put on airs, and show themselves correct in style and deportment in order to reveal themselves utterly and completely. They present themselves and unmask themselves at the same time.

So let us not carp and cavil if they wear the buskins, make exalted speeches, and don magnificent robes and wigs, for their solemnity has a deep meaning. A breath of the old religious consecration, an inwardness of soul, and a remembrance of man's divine sonship and eternal dignity dwell in them, enlarging, heightening, and ennobling them. And this quality acts, sometimes more and sometimes less powerfully and genuinely, in the whole style of this body of drama, which nowadays is only too often misunderstood and derided as stylized, conventional, and intellectual.

Their Value

Our next task is to determine the value of this literature, now that some of the shadows that threatened to obscure it have been dispelled. Racine, his contemporaries, and posterity have always agreed that the strength of his work lay in his stage pieces and not in the few chance lyrical, epigrammatic, and miscellaneous writings. His poetry functions as indirect speech; hence it is more representation than direct personal expression, and for this very reason must be considered as a form complete in itself. There is little sense in breaking it up into the biography and the psychology of its creator. It is self-sufficient, and its relation to reality is that of the spectacle, from beginning to end. I know of no place where this state of things has been interrupted or even obscured. Nowhere is there an overlap or a breakthrough from the stage to the world, or vice versa. On no account are the boards deserted; the illusion of the theater is never destroyed for the sake of surprise or any other effect. Not even those reflections of the theater on the theater, so beloved of the Baroque period; no indeterminate deepening or lengthening of the scenic space; no boxing in, no perspectives are to be found. The poet has sternly forbidden himself any change of scene lest "*la sainte austérité de ses plaisirs*" be dimmed. In this darkroom all the light emanates from the things and people portrayed, and streams through the auditorium into our minds.

What is this marvelously self-illuminating quality that Racine's characters incorporate and emit? It must surely be an active, self-propelling force, hence a will, but one that must not expend itself on its individual purposes or in the external dramatic action. If it did, it would not be blind, it is true, but it would not shine forth in the persons, in its own bearers, but rather in its successes, its sacrifices, and its victories, somewhat as in heroic epic, for instance, or in history, where deeds and achievements, not individual human beings, really hold the stage. It must be a will that has been broken, rejected, or taken back, a thwarted, impeded, miscarried regretted action that—instead of comprehending its purpose and reaching its goal—backfires and kindles devouring flames in the breast of its creator.

Hence the dramatic object of this body of drama is always failure in some guise. The heroes are unfortunate, and this gives the plays a fundamentally tragic note. Even the comedy *Les Plaideurs* is based on the thwarted, suspended impetus of the will, on misadventure and misfortune. In the two religious plays, *Esther* and *Athalie,* God's warriors achieve success only because they are actuated not by their own individual, personal will but by a common, higher one. Hence these prophetlike people, Esther and Joad, are not subject to the law of the closed space of the stage. They are not self-illuminating; they stand, so to speak, under a light from above. In *Esther* the scene changes from act to act; in *Athalie* the background finally opens and one looks into the Holy of Holies of the Temple as into the jaws of eternity. "Here the back of the stage opens up. One sees the interior of the temple; and the armed Levites emerge on the scene from all sides." These two exceptions serve to confirm how intergrown the outer and inner perceptions are in these dramas.

Yet all this could be quite pointless, were it merely a matter of the portrayal of human failures. Anyone to whom only failure has meaning will find satire or world-weary lyric poetry more to his taste. Of course we have sometimes noted outbursts of satire and world-weariness in Racine's life and writings, too. His nobler and more authentic works, however, show that the real value of failure is the self-examination that it evokes in great natures. If we have shown failure to be the dramatic theme of his compositions, we must at the same time recognize the place of self-examination as its motive force, its real inspiration.

This fact, it seems to me, brings us to the basic problem facing the literary critic in the work of Racine: how is his inspiration, human self-examination, compatible with his theme, human failure? If we pass the various dramas in review, bearing this question in mind, we shall perhaps succeed in grasping their literary value.

The Individual Dramas

LA THÉBAÏDE

In his very first work, *La Thébaïde,* the dramatic theme is grasped resolutely. One could not ask, in any tragic drama, for more tragedy than is here packed into twenty-four hours in a royal palace. The enemy brothers, Etéocle and Polynice, kill each other. Their cousin Hémon dies trying to separate them, their younger cousin, Ménecée, having already sacrificed his life in a vain effort to bring about their reconciliation. Their mother, Jocaste, and their sister, Antigone, kill themselves, and their uncle, the intriguer Créon, collapses after failing to kill himself, so that finally, of all the characters on the stage, only the confidants and the messengers are still on their feet. In his more mature years Racine himself realized that tragedy had been piled on a little too heavily here. "The catastrophe in my play is perhaps a bit too gory. In fact, there seems hardly an actor in it who does not die in the end, but after all, it is the Thébaïde, the most tragic subject in antiquity," he writes in his Preface of 1676. But it was just this all-embracing tragedy that seemed to make the material, recommended by some perceptive friends, attractive to him.

Racine's own particular inspiration, the idea of self-examination, can hardly find expression here for sheer wealth of material and depth of misfortune. Imitation, which recalls Euripides, Seneca, Rotrou, and above all Corneille, is the predominant note here. Nevertheless, the Racinian flame flickers, if at first faintly, in the figure of Antigone, who stands alone in clearheaded thoughtfulness amid the storm of passions:

> Et toi seule verses des larmes,
> Tous les autres versent du sang (V, 1)

> And you alone shed tears, all others shed blood

she says to herself, and

> Mais laissez-moi, de grâce, un peu de solitude (V, 3)

> But I beg of you, leave me to myself a bit

to Créon; and while her brothers fight each other furiously in single combat:

> Infortunés tous deux, dignes qu'on vous déplore!
> Moins malheureux pourtant que je ne suis encore,
> Puisque, de tous les maux qui sont tombés sur vous,
> Vous n'en sentez aucun, et que je les sens tous. . . . (V, 2)

> Two unfortunates worthy of pity! But less wretched than I am since you feel none of the woes that have befallen you, and I feel them all....

To which one may mentally add the lines that Racine struck out later:

Quand on est au tombeau, tous nos tourments s'apaisent;
Quand on est furieux, tous nos crimes nous plaisent;
Des plus cruels malheurs le trépas vient à bout;
Le fureur ne sent rien, mais la douleur sent tout. (V, 2)

When one is in the grave all torments are calmed. When one is furious, all our crimes are appealing. Death puts an end to the cruelest woes; fury feels nothing, but pain feels all.

Moreover, all the reflection, all the reasoning, of the characters is at the service of their passionate desires, and the heroes hold forth with Corneille-like rhetoric and firmness as advocates of themselves. Only when they meet resistance and burst out in sudden exasperation do we once more hear the voice of nature and that failure of the spirit in face of the rebellious instincts, that abdication and submersion of reason that Racine feels and expresses no less vividly than its dawning and its resplendence. An example of such nocturnal brilliance, as it were, in which the demon stirs in man, is the passage in which Etéocle bursts out against the demands of his mother:

Hé bien, Madame, hé bien, il faut vous satisfaire:
Il faut...
Il faut...
Il faut...
Il faut par mon trèpas... (I, 3)

Well then, Madame, well then, to satisfy you it is necessary: It is necessary... it is necessary... it is necessary... It is necessary by my death...

or where Créon, with à violent gesture, tears himself away from Antigone:

Je le ferai, Madame; et je veux par avance
Vous épargner encor jusques à ma présence

I will do it, Madame, and now I want to spare you even my presence, and especially in the great scene of the fourth act, where the brothers launch into abuse of each other in the presence of their mother:

POLYNICE: Tu sais qu'injustement tu remplis cette place.
ETÉOCLE: L'injustice me plaît, pourvu que je t'en chasse....
POLYNICE: Et moi je ne veux plus, tant tu m'es odieux,
Partager avec toi la lumière des cieux.
JOCASTE: Allez donc, j'y consens, allez perdre la vie.

POLYNICE: I know that you unjustly fill that place.
ETÉOCLE: The injustice suits me, provided that I drive you from it....
POLYNICE: And as for me, I find you so odious that I no longer want to share the light of the heavens with you.
JOCASTE: Go then, I consent, go lose your lives.

These, and some other passages, although rather inadequate in a literary sense, suffice, if not to free the whole from the dramatic system of Corneille, and more especially from the obvious model of *Horace*, at least to indicate a new direction: in the *Thébaïde*, the conflict between fatherland and inclination, honor and love, is restricted to the peripheral action involving Hémon, Antigone, and Créon. In its place something quite different comes to the fore, not a struggle between incompatible ideals, but a purely emotional, in fact bestial, hatred between brothers, children born of incest, who know that the curse of nature and of the gods lies upon them. In order to avoid Corneille's drama of conflict, Racine approaches the Greek drama of fate; but it, in turn, failed to provide him with any solution, it inevitably became still another insurmountable obstacle. Actually, the weakest pages of the *Thébaïde* are the motif of the pronouncement of the oracle, the sacrificial death of Ménecée, the deliberate obstinately rhetorical ferocity of the enemy brothers, who are driven by adverse fate, and the theatrical superstition of their mother. Clearly, it is not only Corneille's influence but also Greek archaism that prevents all these characters from beating their own breasts and becoming Racine's spirit incarnate.

ALEXANDRE LE GRAND

With *Alexandre,* Racine's as yet inexperienced muse makes its greatest concession to contemporary taste and to the world in general. It succumbs to the temptations of that belief in human glory that was common in the proximity of the Sun King. The brilliance of Louis XIV in love and war, and Corneille's tragedy *La Mort de Pompée,* which might just as well have been called *César le Grand,*[3] had enthralled our poet. Hence the emergence of a hero on whom fortune smiles equally in war and in love, a hero who is luck personified, and the very embodiment of unlimited ability and achievement. When achievement and good fortune join hands, the result is fame. This whole "tragedy" is a hymn to fame and love; hence nothing could be farther from a tragedy in the present-day sense. All the other characters in it strive after fame and love, honorable love and kindly fame, "dans le noble *transport de cette jalousie*"—in noble rivalry with or against Alexandre. First there is Porus, the Indian prince, who gambles his realm and his life to match his strength against Alexandre and win the loving glances of Queen Axiane, or die in the attempt. The latter, for her part, tries to lure the second Indian Prince, Taxile, into the same arena, with the intention of granting her favor to the one who proves himself the better man. And finally there is Cléophile, who aspires to win the heart of the world conqueror. In short, it is, all around, a large-hearted rivalry, uncalculating and trustful, that sees the height of human achievement in courtly brilliance, gallant heroism, and heroic gallantry, in which each competitor excels the others in *his own* way, and so can imagine himself winning; a competition of ambition that really can be played with festive gaiety and even, to some extent, with smiling faces. For the vanquished one here must certainly be a faint-hearted, inadequate person—not a complete hero. The loser is Taxile, and it is difficult for the onlooker to take his death tragically, though the poet seems to have meant it that way. The drama vacillates between a festal and a tragic attitude, and only the nobility and purity of the language can cloak the uncertainty of conception. No doubt Racine had to imitate his contemporaries before he was able to find his own particular path. Moreover, one cannot see in his *Alexandre* much more than a work of homage to the king, who was fond of having himself painted by Le Brun as Alexander. But the beauty of the verse is undeniable, and the vivid expression of the injured, jealous, exasperated spirit, athirst for success and happiness, is even more astounding here, in this second effort, than in the *Thébaïde*.

TAXILE: Il faut que tout périsse ou que je sois heureux. (IV, 4)

. . . .

PORUS: La gloire est le seul bien qui nous puisse tenter,
Et le seul que mon cœur cherche à lui disputer;
C'est elle . . . .

EPHESTION (*en se levant*):
Et c'est aussi ce que cherche Alexandre. (II, 2)

TAXILE: All must perish, or I must be happy.

. . . .

PORUS: Glory is the only good that can tempt us, and the only one that my heart disputes him; it is glory. . . .

EPHESTION (getting up): It is also what Alexander seeks.

ANDROMAQUE

According to the general verdict, *Andromaque* is the first work of really high quality, and represents Racine's spirit and art so completely that one can follow, as clearly articulated parts, the two moving principles of his work, his dramatic sense of the tragic and his contemplative inwardness, and see them personified in the antithesis of Andromaque and Hermione. These two female characters dominate the drama and confront each other as lyric and dramatic voices, respectively. Andromaque, completely inward, preserving the memory of Troy and of her Hector in her heart, protecting the life of her one little son, seems a Hellenic version of the *pietas*, almost unmoved in the midst of a tumult of strange passions and linked to life by her maternal anxiety. One might think this an undramatic figure, and for a time the author too feared that it was. For in his first version (1668) he made Andromaque reappear in the last act so that she could take a decisive stand regarding the murder of her protector and torturer Pyrrhus and the rescue of her child. Later he realized how superfluous it was to drag into the limelight once more the woman who, even in her painful protective custody and captivity, is still the real and powerful, if involuntary, motive force behind the whole drama. The daring and originality of the conception lies precisely in the fact that a suffering creature, by her pure spirituality and fidelity and without use of any female wiles whatsoever,[4] arouses in her environment an all-destroying storm of passions and crimes from which she alone emerges, a silent victor. The various situations and developments through which this is ultimately achieved are comparatively unimportant in themselves, as Racine himself realized and stated in his second prologue, where he cited Joachim Camerarius in answering his critics: "It is not at all necessary to amuse oneself by carping at the poets for changes they have made in the fable; one should, instead, devote one's energies to considering the excellent use they have made of these changes, and the ingenious manner in which they have succeeded in accommodating the fable to their subject."

The subject is in fact this self-effacing, self-sacrificing, protecting Andromaque, "Captive, always sad, a nuisance to myself," although of the four chief characters she has the scantiest part to play. The quiet change that takes place in her is the spiritual mainspring of the drama. In the beginning she appears stormy, proud, distrustful, outraged; she always feels herself menaced and ill-used, and relates everything to herself. People have designs on her child's life, yet she can think of herself:

> Hélas! on ne craint point qu'il venge un jour son père;
> On craint qu'il n'essuyât les larmes de sa mère...
> Mais il me faut tout perdre, et toujours par vos coups...
> Et vous n'êtes pas tous deux connus que par mes larmes....
> (I, 4)

> Alas! they do not fear that he will one day avenge his father, but rather that he will dry his mother's tears... but I must lose all, and always at your hands... and both of you are known only by my tears.

In her distress having learned how to plead, she clasps the knees of her lord though she still hates him as the son of Achilles and the bloody conqueror of Troy. Then, as she prays at Hector's grave, a change comes over her, making her gentle and confirming her in the "innocent guile" of her love, by which she saves her child and, in an unexpected way, herself too. The Christian religion would not have inspired her with the decision to commit suicide; yet her piety, compounded as it is of renunciation, forgiveness, and self-sacrifice, is Christian in tone; it is cloaked in classical antiquity, which frees it of ecclesiastical narrowness and makes it, humanly speaking, all the more inward. The prayerful scene at the grave, the decisive scene, which is not portrayed on the stage, can be sensed from Andromaque's last wish for her son:

> Mais qu'il ne songe plus, Céphise, à nous venger:
> Nous lui laissons un maître, il le doit ménager.
> Qu'il ait de ses aïeux un souvenir modeste. (IV, 1)

> But, Céphise, he must no longer dream of avenging us; we leave him a master whom he must humor. Let him think modestly of his ancestors.

All else that occurs in the five acts gives the impression of being a somber accompaniment to this heavenly song and a sensual echo of it. The play of intrigue that emanates from Hermione must be evaluated for its spiritual significance rather than its practical dramatic usefulness. The external situation is as confused and dilemmatic as a dream. The relationships of the four main characters do not involve real-life power and prestige in the full and historical sense but, rather, power politics of the heart and mind; and this inner conflict between person and person, woman and man, is embodied in the rarefied forms of courtly manners and behavior—the behavior growing increasingly rarefied as the conflict grows more serious. With Racine, the struggle for life between minds takes the illusionistic form of play—usually involving the point of honor and gallantry—not because the conflict is felt feebly or playfully but because it must not be distorted by entanglement with the common human interests of money and possessions.

Hermione, the woman who cannot and will not renounce and forgive, who in her injured pride deliberately loses all sense of proportion, and who blindly prepares the way for her own destruction by her overweening desire to dominate, is therefore the reverse of Andromaque—through her nature much more than her actions. She is Andromaque's poetic contrast rather than her dramatic opponent. In the only scene in which she could argue things out with Andromaque (III, 4) she evades a showdown and has hardly a thing to say except the dry and scornful words: "Je conçois vos douleurs" (I can imagine your suffering).

Thus the drama might have reduced itself to the portrayal of two female characters bound together only by an impressive contrast of tone, if Oreste and Pyrrhus had not also been portrayed with external unity. Their dramatic function requires that the action of the drama—the interplay of fate and chance, and their own deeds, and the courtly rules of this game—receives more emphasis than does their individuality as human beings. Pyrrhus has been betrothed to Hermione for reasons of state, but he cannot bring himself to marry her because he loves Andromaque. Instead of solving the deadlock by the effort of his own will, he transfers it to Andromaque, forcing the defenseless woman to choose between marriage with him and the death of her child. This is the dual pivot on which the play turns, and is also its weak spot, but we must accept it as it is and believe and feel with the author. It is the traditional fiction and fable, without which no poetical happening could be won from reality. Therefore one must not blame the character of the magnanimous Pyrrhus for the pressure that he brings to bear on Andromaque. The critics who find this character badly drawn or contradictory should heed the explanation given in the very first scene of the first act:

> Il l'aime...
> Il fait couler des pleurs, qu'aussitôt il arrête...
> ....
> Ainsi n'attendez pas que l'on puisse aujourd'hui
> Vous répondre d'un cœur si peu maître de lui.
>
> He loves her... he makes her tears flow and immediately staunches them...
> ....
> Therefore do not expect that you will today be given assurances by a heart so little master of itself.

He is a strong man, but caught and portrayed in his weak moment, that is to say, illumined and at the same time overshadowed by the two women between whom that *aujourd'hui* places him, thrilled and infected by the spiritual qualities now of the one, now of the other, to such a degree that his manliness can now only show itself in his outer bearing as a sense of honor and as gallantry. He is an Alexander the Great whom fortune has delivered up to tragedy. And his tragedy strikes him, with Oreste's dagger, in the heart, his only vulnerable part.

Oreste stands utterly and completely on the side of darkness, bemused and bewitched by Hermione, and incapable of decision. He is at once her tool and her victim. Any capacity for reflection or thought that he can summon up only draws him deeper and deeper into bondage and drives him to madness. Recollection only helps to strengthen his chains by convincing him that his love for Hermione is his destiny.

> Puisqu'après tant d'efforts ma résistance est vaine,
> Je me livre en aveugle au destin qui m'entraîne. (I, 1)

> And since after so many efforts my resistance is futile,
> I blindly give myself up to the destiny that leads me.

At first Racine had written *au transport qui m'entraîne*. But by raising the natural instinct to the metaphysical plane, he inflates the lovelorn weakling into a demonic criminal, leading him step by step from his romantic obsession to a criminal obsession. It is precisely self-consciousness, the philosophy of passion, that sets this Céladon beside himself, drives him to assassination, and brings on him all the horrors of an outraged conscience. He would have remained harmless had he meditated less zealously on the inclination of his heart.

Hand in hand with the blinding confusion of love goes the sweet self-reflection of his ego until he sees his "fate fulfilled" and loses his reason through his own self-distortion.

This thrilling tragedy, with its spiritual black-and-white art, moves from Andromaque's growing clarity of mind to the complete mental derangement of Oreste. Its restrained speech indicates, now by veiled language and allusion, now by lightning flashes and deep-cast shadows, the finest dawn and sunset shades of the human spirit, and leaves it to the actor to apply the coloring that best suits the chaste tone. Because of their artistic economy of language, their alleged lack of picturesqueness and color, and their actual exactitude of expression, *Andromaque* and all the other great dramas of Racine confront the actor with the most rewarding and most difficult of tasks.

LES PLAIDEURS

I should be afraid to follow *Andromaque* with an examination of *Les Plaideurs* if this comedy had merely a biographical connection with the tragedies and not a literary one too. If *Les Plaideurs* only imitated Aristophanes, only poked fun at the French love of litigation, mocked and annoyed a few contemporaries, amused a few friends of the author's youth, and represented only a capricious wish to try his hand at comedy, we would be justified in leaving the piece alone. For in that case it would be an isolated work that proved nothing more than its author's cleverness, wit, supremely good stagecraft, and command of language, particulary of the alexandrine.

But it is in fact dominated by the same view of life and of humanity as *Andromaque,* or *Bajazet,* or *Mithridate,* even if not by the same mood. It constitutes a transposition from the tragic voice to the ludicrously comic one, in which the Racinian line and melody are adhered to, and its effect is something like that which would be produced if a Wagnerian baritone were to sing falsetto, or a painter of tragic scenes from history were to do drawings for a comic magazine. The handwriting remains the same; everything else is skillfully disguised. The three chief comic characters, Perrin Dandin the judge, Chicanneau the bourgeois, and Jolande Cudasne, Comtesse de Pimbesche, are no less obsessed by their specific passions than are, for instance, Oreste and Hermione. Their daftness has the typical Racinian characteristic of being unflinching, heroic, and demonic; only in this case it is a petty daftness, a pedantry grown mechanical.

C'est dommage: il avoit le cœur trop au métier

It's too bad: his heart was too taken with his profession

is said of Dandin. He can no longer eat, drink, or sleep, and can do nothing but talk law all the time and everywhere. And when he is advised to moderate his zeal, he replies: "Je veux être malade" (I want to be ill). Yet it is not justice, but its apparatus and formalism that is so close to his heart. He becomes a demon for work, a *perpetuum mobile* of forensic oratory, which, as an empty end in itself, is the very breath of life to him. He is nothing but a temperament without reason or self-command—cattish, incalculable, startling, even crafty, clever, and instinctively sure within the cage of his mania, an uncanny little horror, a Mithridates shrunken to fit into fool's garb and grown fidgety. Such a character could inspire us with horror if he were allowed to give full vent to his passion. The words in the closing scene,

> N'avez vous jamais vu donner la question? . . .
> Bon! Cela fait toujours passer une heure ou deux,

> Have you never seen anyone put to the question? . . .
> Good! It always helps to pass an hour or two,

give us a glimpse into an abyss of dehumanization. But the demon is captured, chaffed, and led by the nose, and the inner action consists in this alone—this superb mockery of the demon of litigation personified.

Hence the whole play is based, not on real action, nor yet on spiritual development, but only on the simulated action of hoaxing. The love story of Léandre and Isabelle winds its way like a humorous pretext around this, and serves as a framework that ensures the unity of the whole, in a light, easy vein. Léandre and Isabelle are sketched as unobtrusively as possible; they are merry and almost humorous characters whose happy dispositions and healthy sincerity would seem to originate in farcical comedy or in Molière rather than from Racine's poetical world. On Racine's own admission[5] the little work would probably never have been completed without the suggestions and help of others.

But the imagination with which something inwardly passive and morbid, such as the obsessiveness and devilish trickery of the three main characters, is transposed into uncommonly live action provoked from outside is definitely original Racine. All kinds of hindrances and outbursts, double-crossings and over-reachings, in word and action, are introduced here as humorous patter, the fool's play and tomfoolery accompanying the inner urge to appear important. The lamed reason, the obstinacy of the protagonists' disputatiousness, in itself so dreary, is turned into pure knockabout comedy.

The play is a joke concerning someone with an irresistible love of litigation who enters the fray armed with all the weappons and formulas of the law, stumbles over his own trickery, is held up by trifling chance incidents, and, having made a fool of himself, is shown up in the end as the worthless idiot that he is. Anyone who has seen *Les Plaideurs* on a French stage will always remember two particular scenes as the highest comedy: first, the interrupted plea in the second act and, second, the parodied trial in the third. The first time everything goes so briskly and everyone is so intent on his aim that no one has a chance to make himself heard, because all are trying to speak at the same time; the second time the pleading is so long-winded and pompous that it puts the most zealous of all judges to sleep. This knockabout comedy is expressed both adventurously and naturally even in the treatment of the verse, with its breaks and interlinking, its suppressions and accelerations, and its astonishing rhymes. Thre is something of both pantomime and the ballet about *Les Plaideurs*, although neither ballet nor mime enters into the piece.

The characters are not persons; they are possessed souls who dance the dance of fools. The only circumspect man among them, Petit Jean the porter, who speaks a kind of prologue at the beginning and ultimately becomes entangled himself in the gibberish of forensic eloquence, is a cunning boor.

> Ma foi, sur l'avenir bien fou qui se fîra:
> Tel qui rit vendredi, dimanche pleurera.
> ....
> Ma foi, juge et plaideurs, il faudroit tout lier.

> On my word, he who puts his faith in the future is mad: the man who laughs on Friday will weep on Sunday.
> ....
> On my word, judge and litigants should all be tied up.

These are the aphorisms of his truth; they express thoughtfulness and inwardness in such a droll way that one might say

Racine's muse had reversed its own laws of life and its own style in every way. It has shown up the passionate person as a fool and the thoughtful person as blockhead. The muse has delighted for a brief moment in this caricature, forged its strength on it, made sure of its ability in this genre, and above all, tested its own beliefs by means of this foil. For it is clear now that the things of the world have a meaning for Racine only in the tragic view, since the comical view produced only an empty emotion, a pantomime in words, a comical imaginary existence, instead of a natural picture full of vigor.

Jules Lemaître says: "For my part, I am sorry that Racine did not write other comedies besides *Les Plaideurs.*"[6] No doubt his *Plaideurs* is a masterpiece of humor, high spirits, and audacity, but in the intellectual calendar of our poet's life span, carnival came only once.

BRITANNICUS and BAJAZET

In time sequence *Britannicus* and *Bajazet* are separated from one another by *Bérénice.* In spite of this, they belong together for our consideration, because the same general shifting of the poetic center of gravity occurs in each. Racine doubtless felt that light and movement should emanate from the titular heroes Britannicus and Bajazet in each case, as it did from *Andromaque.* In fact, however, the poetical life, in Racine's imagination, revolves, not around the innocent, oppressed persons, but around the oppressors, the executioners, the fighters, Néron, Agrippine, Roxane, and Acomat. Political and criminal natures are beginning to fascinate the poet more than the patiently suffering, self-sacrificing ones. This secularization of his muse, like most processes of secularization, was definitely not intentional, but having proved successful with a Hermione, it was not unnatural. The spectacle of the sensual, passionate person grown violent through passion, weakness, and thirst for power inevitably and naturally impressed Racine as the richer and dramatically more rewarding spectacle. This demanded more objectivity in his future works, more earthy realism; hence it pointed to historical material, and set Racine to work with industry and eager curiosity in pursuit of tragic events historically documented. His *Britannicus* is full of concrete features and details from Tacitus, Seneca, and Suetonius. "Here is the one of my tragedies that I can say I have toiled at the most," he says with reason,[7] for none of the others is as heavily documented as this one.

The documentation of *Bajazet* is less historical in the scholarly sense, it is true, but it must have struck Racine's contemporaries as all the more palpable and convincing for the general understanding, bacause for this "*pourtant très-véritable*" subject Racine was able to draw on personal accounts and living authorities. A friend of the French ambassador in Constantinople had given him a circumstantial account of the whole course of events.

Such dependence on external reality and authorities, such assured credibility and authenticity, is, by nature, always somewhat inimical to poetry, for it has to be worked out and thus it makes the writer's task more difficult rather than easier. The better documented the crimes, intrigues, malicious tricks, and passions of an Agrippina or a Roxana or a Nero are, and the more convincingly the innocence of a Britannicus or a Bajazet can be proved by history, the more prosaic they must inevitably become.

If the psychology of crime or of innocence sufficed to make them poetical, then these two tragedies would certainly be among Racine's highest achievements, for the mastery of the psychological study in both dramas is beyond question. The characters' motives and actions in these plays have been so often dissected and reassembled, observed and extolled, that I could scarcely add anything new. Besides, I would be wary of casting the slightest doubt on Racine's penetration and prudence. His sense of spiritual and historical reality has reached its full maturity here. But all this has only about as much to do with literature as the dissection of a body has with its animation or the understanding of an event with its portrayal. It is the prosaic preparation for a flight of the imagination. Not that this flight did not take place. How could it have failed to do so after such thorough provisions were made for it? Only it seems to me that it did not quite reach the intended height, that the downfall of Britannicus and of Bajazet, while definitely conceivable, indeed understandable, and to a large extent even obvious, has nevertheless not become self-evident. The poetical is self-evident and compelling. And these very protagonists and their fate lack this magic something. One does not believe, one does not see, that for young men such as Bajazet and Britannicus—inoffensive people, who could live happily in a nutshell—there should be no way out, no rescue, no breath of life here below. In fact, it is only the artificial thread of chance that decides whether they may not, after all, yet escape from the grasp of their oppressor.

They both have something of Hamlet about them, although their indecisive reflection remains outside of them; hence, instead of gripping us, it makes us impatient. They are prone to dilemmas, not to problems, and the anemic pallor of their thought is only theatrical make-up. Hence one cannot even assert with confidence that something such as laming of the will by the conscience, or renunciation through greatness of soul, in short, something Hamlet-like, was present in the poet's mind as he portrayed them. *Britannicus* is reminiscent of Hamlet only because the hero finds himself excluded from his position as rightful successor to the throne. Moreover, he seems too young, too honorable, and too naïve to be brooding and mistrustful. But at the same time he is aware that his youthful trustfulness is beautiful, and he carries this blindness before him like a letter of recommendation. From one side he shows himself as a tough young fellow, from another side as soppy and precocious. When that archrogue and villain Narcisse remarks,

> C'est à vous de choisir des confidents discrets,
> Seigneur, et de ne pas prodiguer vos secrets,

> It's up to you to choose discreet confidants, my lord, and not to scatter your secrets about,

he replies:

> Narcisse, tu dis vrai. Mais cette défiance
> Est toujours d'un grand cœur la dernière science. (I, 4)

> Narcisse, you speak truly. But such suspicion is always learned late by a generous heart.

With self-satisfied naïveté he trips along to death:

> Adieu, je vais, le cœur tout plein de mon amour,
> Au milieu des transports d'une aveugle jeunesse,
> Ne voir, n'entretenir que ma belle princesse.
> Adieu. (V, 1)

> Farewell. My heart full of love, amidst the transports of blind youth I will see and speak to none but my beautiful princess. Farewell.

Precious characters cannot be tragic.

Bajazet, with his half-guilt and his half-conscience, has something almost pharisaical about him. His pensive sincerity justifies and elucidates itself at such lengths that finally the hearer no longer wants to believe it and becomes tired of this toying with veracity. Nevertheless there is no doubt that these eponymous heroes, who give such a painful impression, were meant to figure in the respective works as models of greatness of soul. When a man of action such as the old Grand Vizier Acomat says of Bajazet,

> O courage inflexible! O trop constante foi,
> Que même en périssant j'admire malgré moi! (II, 3)

> O inflexible courage! O too constant faith, that even in perishing I admire in spite of myself!

and when, in the eighth scene of the third act, Britannicus can rise so high above Néron, one would surely assume that the poet was seriously intent on awarding these youths the palm for beauty of soul. But literature disposed matters otherwise and recognized as its true children and favorites Néron, Agrippine, Roxane, and Acomat. These demonically inspired people put those elegant and seraphic puppets in the shade. But since their intended place within the compass of the play was not quite the forefront, they burst open the dramatic framework and forcibly draw upon themselves, upon their spiritual situation alone, the gaze of the onlooker. The play about the fortunes of Britannicus and Junie becomes a portrayal of Néron's degeneracy and Agrippine's depravity, and the rivalry accompanying the elevation to the throne and coronation of Bajazet and Atalide becomes a psychological story of Roxane's passion and a monument to Acomat's resolution. One looks beyond what is happening on the stage and into an epic world in which a Néron finds room to give vent to his passions, an Acomat to stand up to a test, a Roxane and an Agrippine to rule and make a bad job of it. The sultry air of the Roman imperial court and of the Ottoman harem is so natural and convincing as the native element of Néron and Roxane that one is no longer willing to believe and look on as Britannicus and Bajazet smother in it—they have become only too well acclimatized to it, thanks to their precious and artificial characters.

Hence the continued influence exerted by these works, when traced through literary history, must be sought and will be found more frequently in the novel—in the art of describing a milieu and the psychology of its characters—rather than in the forms of dramatic composition. This applies in a certain sense to all of Racine's plays.[8] For the deepest emotion with which they are all more or less imbued is renunciation; and the art of extracting drama from a negative action has remained Racine's inalienable secret.

BÉRÉNICE

If we approach Racine's dramatic art expecting to penetrate its secret through the school concept of dramatic technique, we are making things unduly easy for ourselves. We take his *Bérénice,* place it alongside old Corneille's *Tite et Bérénice* written at the same time, look at it, and see bow both authors have set about coping with the same task and the same material. For both deal with the same subject—the renunciation of the promptings of the heart for reasons of state—and even the same historical personages. This much, we think, is surely quite clear.

Although such formal, comparative criticism is the wrong track, we must follow it to the end, deducing from it the technique used in each case, in order to convince ourselves how far afield it is of the true *Bérénice* of Racine. Renunciation, it is said, is neither a direct action nor an effect, but only a restraint of our impulses, and for this reason it is, by its very nature, little suited to dramatic treatment. To be just, one must therefore allow both Racine and Corneille the mitigating circumstances of the unfavorable character and inflexible nature of the material. In the grammar of our thought, "drama" signifies an active form, and the fact that renunciation naturally cannot fit into this category was recognized neither by Corneille nor by Racine. One can write idylls or elegies about acts of renunciation and resignation—according to the critics of the formal school—or turn them into a historical novel, as Madame de Lafayette did in her *Princesse de Clèves* (1678), but surely not into a drama in the true sense.

But now Corneille was ingenious enough to hold the Emperor Titus, the one who has ultimately to make the greatest renunciation, in suspense and keep him dangling, as it were, for four acts. To do this he needed another figure as the mainspring and ballistic force of the action, and he found it in Domitie, with her urge to domineer. She loves Domitien, the brother of Tite (the Emperor Titus), but she also longs to be empress. Therefore she makes love to Tite, too, at the same time. Always fixed on her one goal, the throne, she is equally ready to give her hand to Domitien, to compass the downfall of Tite, or to desert Domitien in order to become empress with Titus. She knows exactly what she wants, and says it plainly and straightly to Domitien's face:

> Mon cœur va tout à vous quand je le laisse aller.
> Mais, sans dissimuler j'ose aussi vous le dire,
> Ce n'est pas mon dessein qu'il m'en coûte l'empire;
> Et je n'ai point une âme à se laisser charmer
> Du ridicule honneur de savoir bien aimer.
> La passion due trône est seule toujours belle,
> Seule à qui l'âme doive une ardeur immortelle. (I, 2)

> My heart goes to you, when I give it free rein, but to hide nothing from you let me tell you that it is not my purpose to let my heart cost me the empire; and my soul is not one to allow itself to be charmed by the ridiculous honor of knowing how to love well. Passion for the throne alone is always beautiful, the only passion to which the soul owes an immortal ardor.

In her lover, on the other hand, the pure will to love is the ruling force; he strives for her hand, with or without the imperial throne. Hence these two want something definite, and what they want is ultimately realized, for the matter is settled when Domitie gives Domitien her hand and he is recognized as coruler with Tite, and his successor. Up to this there is not a trace of renunciation. But what becomes of Bérénice? She, too, is no patient sufferer, but, to an even greater degree than Domitie, a vigorous character, greedy for power. On receiving a hint from a confidant, she makes a surprise appearance in Rome in order to remind the emperor, a few days before he is due to be married to Domitie, of her prior rights and to take possession of his hand, his heart, his throne, and indeed his mind. For she sets the utmost value on intellectual recognition and domination. As long as the reason of state, that is to say, *Senatus populusque romanus,* is opposed to her union with Titus, she seeks by every means to get her way, but when she is granted Roman citizenship and is recognized and honored, when all obstacles have been overcome, she suddenly renounces the victim of her moral conquest with magnanimity and cleverness. The principle and the glory are what she is after. After she has won these and conquered all hearts, she finds it both noble and reasonable to abdicate. "La crainte est amoureuse," she says. "Nous pourrions vivre heureux, mais avec moins de gloire" (Fear is amorous; we could live happily, but with less glory). This Oriental queen is of a rare and regal nature. She does not want to put her luck in politics and love to any further tests in Rome, and she leaves the stage of world domination and the boards of the theater at the same time, radiant and smiling, in the shining light of her triumph. Dazzled by her gesture, Tite, who has constantly vacillated, now gains the strength to be magnanimous in renunciation himself: he makes his brother a gift of a share of his throne, and Domitie's hand. Infected by the acts of will and noble resolves of the others, lifted up by their loftiness, at the end of the play he is, unexpectedly, on the highest peak of heroic greatness of soul. By this very clever, amusing, and surprising treatment of the human will, Corneille has succeeded in making renunciation appear as the most sublime form of our urge to self-assertion.

The critics have shaken their heads and said that this play is not really a tragedy after all, and that, compared with Racine's *Bérénice,* it is a wretched, contrived piece of work. As if Corneille had ever intended his *Tite et Bérénice* to be a tragedy! He calls it simply and straightforwardly a *comédie héroïque,* and his heroic verses are full of comical and ironical undertones.[9] Could anyone have expressed more wittily and more elegantly the moral of the whole thing, the formula of the ordinary love between men and women?

> Seigneur, s'il m'est permis de parler librement,
> Dans toute la nature aime-t-on autrement?
> L'amour-propre est la source en nous de tous les autres;
> C'en est le sentiment qui forme tous les nôtres;
> Lui seul allume, éteint, ou change nos désirs:
> Les objets de nos vœux le sont de nos plaisirs.
> Vous-même, qui brûlez d'une ardeur si fidèle,
> Aimez-vous Domitie, ou vos plaisirs en elle?
> Et quand vous aspirez à des liens si doux,
> Est-ce pour l'amour d'elle, ou pour l'amour de vous? (I, 3)

> My lord, if I may speak freely, in all nature does one love otherwise? Self-love is the source within us of all the others. It is the sentiment that forms all of ours; it alone fires, dampens, or changes our desires: the objects of our vows are those of our pleasures. Yourself, who burn with so faithful a flame, do you love Domitie, or your pleasure in her? And when you aspire to such gentle bonds, is it for love of her, or for love of yourself?

> Seigneur, telle est l'humeur de la plupart des femmes.
> L'amour sous leur empire eût-il rangé mille âmes,
> Elles regardent tout comme leur propre bien,
> Et ne peuvent souffrir qu'il leur echappe rien. (IV, 4)

> My lord, such is the humor of most women. Though love had ranged a thousand souls under their empire, they consider all their personal property. And they cannot bear to allow anything to escape them.

"What! A dissertation on self-love in a tragedy? Have done with that, 'Voltaire exclaims, and then cuts his interpretation short,' for it would be an attempt to outrage the memory of Corneille if one were to dwell upon all the faults of a work in which there is hardly anything but faults." If Voltaire had only noted the title of this work and taken it as a comedy! But that is just the odd thing: from the first production in 1670 onward, all concerned definitely wanted to see *Tite et Bérénice* as a tragedy. For eight days previously, Racine's *Bérénice,* with all its melancholy, had appeared on the stage, and had trodden down firmly in all theater-loving minds the soil on which Corneille was to come and strew his lighter seed. And to this very day the critics have failed to loosen it up again. The two Bérénice plays are still regarded as rival works, although it is in no way certain that they were meant as such by their respective authors.[10]

This alleged rivalry is also harmful to Racine's tragedy, for if one comes from Corneille, one finds, with apparent justification, that it is lacking in dramatic tension, that it is basically an elegy, a psychological picture, or, in fact, an idyll, and only outwardly bears the marks of a stage play, or has been fashioned into one with difficulty.[11]

From its first appearance up to the present day, *Bérénice* has been found, at one time, not tragic enough, at another, not dramatic enough, because the comparison with Corneille has always barred the way to an insight into its own individual life. But one cannot open up two literary worlds with one kind of key, especially when they have as little in common as these have. For it is only according to the letter that the story of Titus and Berenice is the same in the one play as in the other. In Corneille it is a festal competition of *amour-propre* for scepter and fame; in Racine it is heart-rending misery. In the one, renunciation is the somersault of a satiated sense of power, in the other, the withering of all the blooms of life. What has the one to do with the other? Even our assumption, expressed above, that renunciation is an obstructed and unreal form of willing and acting, applies neither to Corneille nor to Racine; for in truth Racine's *Bérénice* is so dramatic through and through, so very much *vicenda tutta interiore* (a completely interior affair), as an Italian critic says,[12] that its whole poetry lies in the accomplishment, enforcement, assertion, and realization of the innermost will. Here the will steps out from the moral conscience as from a background, and accomplishes its cruel work in the glare of the footlights, before everyone. What does it matter if its destructive deed is accomplished only in words, without any daggers being drawn, or swords being crossed, or poisons mixed, since almost every one of these words is a dagger, a sword, a poisoned cup?

It is not that emphasis or other tricks of speech are used. The power of Racine's dramatic words comes from their genuineness and simplicity. The speech of his characters is so transparent and so objective that it attains the maximum effectiveness with sparing intonation, and has no need of any magic deceit, "starkness," pathetic undulations, or crescendoes. The roots of this art of speech lie in the humanistic education of the author's taste and the Jansenistic purification of his mind.

That man should influence his fellows by words and not by force is humane and humanistic, and only in an ethical world is it possible for words alone to have such directly effective power. In an inferior environment they could only secure a like success by such devious means as, for instance, superstition and hocus-pocus. Racine's *Bérénice* keeps absolutely clear of the insincere magic of words so common in present-day literature. To find once more a comparably calm, exalted, and spiritual power of language combined with a comparable depth of suffering and purity of will, one must listen attentively to Goethe's *Iphigenia* or to Tasso. Only here has the combination of evangelical spirituality and classical learning produced a related dramatic style.

The evangelical spirit, in which all sacramental and other ritualistic rites are excluded and the living word alone decides the salvation or loss of the human soul, wears a courtly and pagan garb in *Bérénice*. This spirit is discernible, not in the costumes, nor even in the decor, but only in the action, only in the fact that the heroes renounce their sensuality, their temperament, their most cherished worldly weaknesses and wishes, and become wholly engrossed in something higher. For Titus this higher element is duty to the Roman state, for Berenice it is love for Titus; not the passionately desiring, blind kind of love, but understanding, self-forgetting, helpful love. For Antiochus, there is no unworldly, altruistic mission of this kind to which he could devote himself. His Commagene kingdom and his political alliance with Rome are a decorative adjunct to his life, as it were—not its content. Hence nothing remains to him but fidelity to his feelings for their own sake, that is, for their purity and beauty: friendship for Titus, and a reverent love for Berenice—without hope and without fulfillment. He is the type of the "beautiful soul" that has to live on memory and pine away in yearning because everything earthly repells him and what is higher only beckons to him from an unattainable distance as a form and a beauty to be gazed upon.

Après cinq ans d'amour et d'espoir superflus,
Je pars, fidèle encor quand je n'espère plus. (I, 2)

> After five years of vain love and hope, I leave, still faithful though I no longer hope.

Antiochus is the unreal hero, a gallant and precious ascetic, who can only portray himself but not really purify himself. Hence he, too, only accompanies, promotes, and illustrates the action of the play as a beautiful figure and an ostensible participant in it. Moreover, one knows from the first act onward that while his love will bloom eternally, his hopes have faded in advance. Titus, the great friend in whose shadow he lives, stands between him and his happiness. But between Titus and Bérénice there also arises a wall of division: the Roman people with their laws, customs, traditions, and claims. They will not tolerate a foreign queen by the side of their emperor. A marriage with her is politically impossible now that Titus must ascend the throne. Indeed, according to Roman concepts, it is illicit and contrary to the law. Titus should surely have known that already, but *"qu'un amant sait mal ce qu'il desire !"* From the vantage point of a high office the world does not look the same as when seen from private life.

> J'aimois, je soupirois dans une paix profonde;
> Un autre étoit chargé de l'empire du Monde. . .
> Mais à peine le ciel eut rappelé mon père,
> Dès que ma triste main eut fermé sa paupière,
> De mon aimable erreur je fus désabusé:
> Je sentis le fardeau qui m'étoit imposé;
> Je connus que bientôt, loin d'être à ce que j'aime,
> Il falloit . . . renoncer à moi-même. (II, 2)

> I loved, I sighed in deep peace: another was charged with empire over the world. . . . But scarcely had heaven recalled my father, no sooner had my sad hand closed his eyelids, than I saw my charming error clearly: I felt the weight that was imposed on me; I soon knew that far from belonging to what I love, I had. . .to renounce my very self.

In the clear, strong mind of the young emperor this renunciation is a matter already decided, *res judicata,* from the very day that he took up the reins of government. Otherwise, how could he use such manly language as this?

> Rome observe aujourd' hui ma conduite nouvelle,
> Quelle honte pour moi, quel présage pour elle,
> Si dès le premier pas, renversant tous ses droits,
> Je fondois mon bonheur sur le débris des lois! (II, 2)
>
> Rome sees today my new conduct. What shame for me, what an omen for her, if after the first step, overthrowing all her rights, I were to build my happiness on the ruins of laws!

And now the real tragedy begins for him: he must carry out the sentence of the law against the heart of his beloved and against his own temper. The dramatic accomplishment of this renunciation, not the curious, spectacle-loving observation of the mental anguish that accompanies it, is the real subject of this tragedy. Here we have an ethically political action that must not be brought down to the level of a "psychological study" by means of romantic and naturalistic pathos and sentimentality. Here psychology is at the service of epic poetry, not the other way round.

Now the reaction of the emotions and the will of those involved in this conflict operate so that Bérénice, wrapped up in her love for Titus, at first does not know or see these Roman ideas of what is lawful; then when she is made aware of them, she still does not understand them, and will not see or observe them; in fact, she rejects them as stupid, harsh, inhuman, and barbaric. With Titus, on the other hand, his sense of law, of the power and necessity of the state, and his moral duty in regard to it, become progressively clearer, more inexorable, and for that very reason more painful. In a slow, agonizing struggle two loving human hearts are torn apart by their own resignation, not by *amour-propre.* The things that normally unite people, the voices of duty and of the heart, estrange these two. They are in danger of grievously misunderstanding each other's motives, and this danger arises through the third party, Antiochus, who might perhaps have founded some hopes on their quarreling and parting. But since all three are eminent and estimable people, external catastrophe is avoided and all the unhappiness is turned inward; the result is mental suffering almost unendurable in its intensity, which brings each of them in turn to the brink of suicide. But each time the pleading of the other person, consideration for him, prevents this final step. And so they come to terms with the affliction they have caused one another, and though their hearts bleed from the renunciation, they go their different ways without hatred or reprocah.

The action emanates from Titus, but Bérénice is the chief figure in the play. The Roman demand works against her, an innocently loving girl. Hence she appears as the touchingly defenseless victim until, goaded on by pain, she seizes the bridle of events, wins back her power over Titus, and causes him to waver in his resolve. Then rising above this feminine victory to an ethical victory over herself, she hands her friend the crown of thorns. In this way she makes him free and sure of himself once more. Her painful ascent from a child of nature to a heroic woman, the martyrdom of her heart, is the core of the play. Her highest victory is the deepest humility.

> Votre cœur s'est troublé, j'ai vu couler vos larmes,
> Bérénice, Seigneur, ne vaut point tant d'alarmes. . . .

> Your heart became troubled, I saw your tears flow.
> Bérénice, my lord, is not worthy of so much anguish. . . .

Thus renunciation and self-denial are represented as the result of the purest powers of the will, a conquest and a rejection of human weakness, a growth of the ethical personality as it works its way upward from the nature of the temperament. All that is left of the natural man in Titus the statesman is his trepidaton, his human fear and bewilderment at sight of his beloved's tears; in Antiochus, there remain the yearning for happiness, and the restless Oriental melancholy of the disappointed senses. For all the charm and guile of her unbroken, healthy femininity, Bérénice is a pure product of nature, the noble daughter of a distant Semitic race, who does not yet know the terrible god whom she bears in her heart, and must come to Rome to sacrifice herself to him.

But these natural and historical limitations are only lightly indicated. Solitary and detached from their environment, these three main figures converge upon each other. They carry Rome, Palestine, and Syria within themselves—not as a shawl flung around them, or a drapery. Their only confidants are their second selves, not their retinue, and they hardly say a thing to them that they could not, and would not have to, say to themselves. One could describe these confidants as fictitious figures serving stage technique, or psychological midwives of the drama, were it not that they acquire their own legitimate existence when practical questions arise that the individual has to decide, for they always take part in some way and demand to be heard. This is designed to show that in ethical and political questions one can be very lonely, but one is never alone; in fact, our action only acquires ethical and political validity when we incorporate the opinions of others into our will and assimilate them into it. The only problems that we confront alone are those purely theoretical ones that coincide with our own heart-searchings. It is a prejudice, and almost a vice, to imagine that we are alone even in questions of conscience and must master the things of the world from the depths of our own spirit, and to consider spiritual counselors and confidants as superfluous or dangerous.

Racine thinks otherwise, and as each of his heroes is a person of great and powerful will, he surrounds him, not with an idle court that would only serve for display and pomp, but with a kind of general staff who work with him and have their hands full in doing so. To achieve clarity in questions of the heart and of the political organism is the task of practical common sense, not of pure reason; it is not a riddle, but a transaction. Titus knows what he requires of his Paulin and how he is to use him:

> Je veux par votre bouche entendre tous les cœurs,
> Vous me l'avez promis. Le respect et la crainte
> Ferment autour de moi le passage à la plainte;
> Pour mieux voir, cher Paulin, et pour entendre mieux,
> Je vous ai demandé des oreilles, des yeux;
> J'ai mis même à ce prix mon amitié secrète;
> J'ai voulu que des cœurs vous fussiez l'interprête;
> Qu'au travers des flatteurs votre sincérité
> Fît toujours jusqu'à moi passer la vérité.
> Parlez donc. (II, 2)

From your mouth I want to hear all hearts speak. You promised me this. Respect and fear seal me off from complaint; dear Paulin, in order to see and hear better I have asked ears and eyes of you. I even set this as the price of my secret friendship; I wanted you to be the interpreter of hearts, that your sincerity always make truth pass through the flatterers to me. Therefore, speak.

These confidants are solidly behind their masters, and have to bear responsibility as well as good fortune and misfortune with them. Above all in a tragedy, where reflection goes so directly hand in hand with the accomplishment of the self-sacrifice as it does here, every explaining, doubting, warning, or comforting word from their mouths must become either a check or an incentive. In this conflict, this rebellion of conscience against passion, they play a role similar to that of public opinion in a revolution. Hence they fade more and more into the background, as the hour of decision comes nearer.

We have emphasized so strongly the dramatic power, the primitive force, of the ethical distress and conflict because the poet has done so much to soften it, to mitigate it, and to camouflage it with the lighter side of his art, and because so many critics have allowed themselves to be deceived by the classical symmetry, and have failed to give the poet and the man his due because they were so lost in admiration of his artistry.

MITHRIDATE and IPHIGÉNIE

The mental excitement from which such a mighty work of literature had come forth continued to vibrate for a long time in Racine's imagination. He could not get away from Bérénice. Two tragedies that came after her in point of time, *Mithridate* and *Iphigénie*, are under her spell, and are variations on, or elegant vulgarizations of, the main thought of *Bérénice*. Outwardly, that is to say, in the theatrical, not indeed in the literary, sense, one can speak of enhancement and enrichment. The means of presentation almost approach the Baroque, the stage becomes more pompous, more colorful, more festive, and there is a return to that secularization of the drama which we have already observed in *Britannicus* and *Bazajet*.

True, *Bazajet* originated directly after *Bérénice*, but in its nature it is more akin to *Britannicus*. Racine's art does not progress in a straight line, as it were, but revolves around its favorite theme, the renunciation of happiness or of life, treating it at one time as a bitter necessity accomplished under pressure and in so heavy an atmosphere that no free-born soul can breathe in it, at another time rather as the soaring flight of ethical volition. *Thé-*

baïde, Britannicus, and *Bazajet* belong to the former, the depressed world of despotism, whereas the freer heroism is glorified in *Alexandre, Andromaque, Bérénice,* and *Phèdre.* Yet both regions of the spirit belong together, interact, and qualify or restrict each other in freedom of action and in the inexorable progress of events. Therefore one can also place *Mithridate* and *Iphigénie* after *Britannicus* and *Bazajet,* but no doubt the decisive point is that the demoniacal element in *Mithridate* and *Iphigénie* is ultimately made to yield to and serve the heroic.

True, the victory of the heroic will over the demons of passion is not achieved either in *Mithridate* or in *Iphigénie* so clearly and so silently, so unperturbed by chance events and so visibly accompanied by spiritual travail, as in *Bérénice.* The distressful agitation of the fifth act, in which everything is topsy-turvy, and the surprises that follow in reckless profusion, betray a certain uncertainty of the poetical line being taken and enliven the scenic rather than the dramatic picture. Whatever stage managers may say, *Bérénice* is essentially more dramatic than either *Mithridate* or *Iphigénie,* and therefore essentially more tragic as well. The ingenious idea on which these two highly spectacular plays are based—namely, that the demonic forces and passions, in the blindness of their rage and despair, ultimately only help the imperiled heroic will to triumph—is an optimistic holiday rather than everyday faith for Racine, something he may indeed have cherished at times but that definitely did not correspond to his deeper feelings about life.

Racine's contemporaries appreciated the festive and spectacular features of *Mithridate* and *Iphigénie,* and they loved to produce these pieces, and also *Alexandre le Grand,* at court functions because of their effectiveness. If one compares them with *Alexandre,* one can see the immense strides Racine had made in his art in the eight years from 1665 to 1673. The gallant heroism of the earlier period has dropped its high-flown audacity and become more earthy, cautious, shrewd, realistic, political, and weighty. Of all the gallant heroes, of the whole literary Faramond type of the seventeenth century, Mithridate is the character who comes most alive—and this is because he is portrayed in his downfall and not in his rise. Tragedy makes him beautiful, hovers around him and illumines him like a fiery sunset, and since it has its source in events rather than in his conscience, it glorifies and adorns him. He knows and says this himself:

> Mon sort . . .
> Veut d'autres sentiments que ceux de la pitié;
> Et ma gloire, plutôt digne d'être admirée,
> Ne doit point par des pleurs être déshonorée. (V, 5)
>
> My fate . . . requires sentiments other than those of pity; and my glory, worthy of being admired, should not be dishonored by tears.

An Asiatic barbarian, full of wild grandeur and cruelty, who grows from the historical into the legendary rather than the mythical, like the hellenized Asian of his time, he is warmed by Greek yearning, gifted with a tendency to freedom and fantasy, and not incapable of human compassion. He feels himself to be both liberator and dictator of the world. He is boundless in his hatred of the Romans, recklessly daring and magnanimous, cunning and suspicious to the point of baseness, brave and intriguing, enthusiastic, noble-minded yet petty and egotistical, coarse and refined, primitive and decadent, all at the same time.

These contradictions make him true to life, or rather, poetically true and live to our imagination. For such a Mithridate probably never existed. He is the barbarian hero as an elegant and cultured European wishes and imagines him to be, and so makes him. Only of such a person is it credible that, advanced in years and in the most frightful plight, cherishing immense plans of world strategy and politics in his breast, he should be lovelorn as a youth and burning like an Othello for the possession of a Greek girl. The mingling of world politics and gallantry that seems to us so dubious in the French literature of the Baroque period, appears perfectly natural and successful here. It has been raised from the convention of the style of the period to the naturalness of the imagination. Hence the politics no longer appear as intrigue but rather as a passionate, personal will to power, and love no longer as gallantry but as wild lust. Such things could go hand in hand in a barbaric mixture of cultures—but not in Paris. That is to say, they could go hand in hand in Paris only when that chaotic barbarism is brought on to the stage by the magic of a mighty poet. Like Corneille when he evokes old Romans, Racine, when he calls up hellenized barbarians, gets an effect that is "historical" in a far deeper sense than ever conceived by any of the loud-voiced critics and romanticists with their demands for local and period color.

After all, it is asked, how can the characters of a Corneille or a Racine be historically genuine when all agree that they are viewed, absolutely and completely, with the eyes of a Frenchman of the reign of Louis XIV? We pose the counter-question: were those eyes really so blind to human and cultural phenomena? And with what other eyes should Corneille and Racine have worked? With the eyes of a professor of history of the twentieth century? All viewing of the past, however objective and historical it may be, tends to take on subjective lights and shades, and that is just what makes it vivid. The view we obtain of Mithridate and his period through Racine's vision seems to me actually to suffer from an excess of historical objectivity, for the action in this drama is determined by historical forces rather than by subjective and personal traits of the poet and his characters.[13] The Romans' attack, Pharnace's successful flight, the intervention of Xipharès, the incalculable behavior of the troops, the steadfastness of individuals and the panic of the masses, all originate behind the scenes and rush tumultuously from a historical world into the drama, bringing down the hero, whom we have just seen standing before us so full of strength, as a storm tears down a mighty oak. Mithridate's fall has almost the effect of a spectacle of nature, and yet it is true that the trail of destruction that the colossus causes by his fall is more or less incidental.

In his shadow, protected and held down by him, his two sons have grown up, and between these there is Monime, the foreign girl from Greece, whom they all three woo passionately. The younger son, Xipharès, is the youthful image of his father, only less rugged and hard; the other one, Pharnace, has inherited his father's egotism and daring but not his greatness. He is the traitor. The involuntary cause of all the dissension is Monime, one of the most enchanting creatures born of Racine's nostalgia for Greece and for virtuous womanhood, Oppressed in her existence yet enhanced in moral worth by the wildest possible environment, she is capable of coping with any situation, and can even renounce her union with her Xipharès as long as her human dignity is not touched. But when Mithridate has torn the womanly secret from her heart by base dissimulation, she breaks with him and prepares to die. At this point events bring the tyrant crashing to the ground. He falls, but he has no wish to crush the pair of lovers in his fall, and Monime's happiness seems just as much a gift of fortune as of Mithridate's magnanimity. The melancholy and heroic basic spirit of readiness to die that permeates all the characters—and Monime in particular—would have led one to expect that the lovers would go under. But then that would have spoiled the theatrically spectacular beauty of Mithridate's fall.

The hybrid character of *Iphigénie,* half tragedy and half ceremonial play, is still more hampering in its effect. Racine came to this subject lured on by his passion for the archaic and the ceremonious, yet cherishing the *Bérénice* mood in his heart. How could he have coped with it successfully except by adaptation and compromise? The tactful and learned poet has lavished a wealth of flexible artistic and linguistic beauties on his Iphigénie, "*qui est une héroïne merveilleusement bien élevée*"[14] (who is a marvelously well brought up heroine), to make up for her literary weakness. And how cleverly he has got around the difficult obstacle of the human sacrifice, to his own satisfaction.[15] All this could pass unnoticed here, since we are dealing with literary values, were it not that the horticultural art of grafting old Greek myths onto new French thought has produced an uncommonly strong shoot in the figure of Eriphile, whose suicide is so arbitrarily and ingeniously inserted in the place of Iphigénie's sacrifice. She is an obvious preliminary study for Phèdre:

> J'ignore qui je suis, et pour comble d'horreur,
> Un oracle effrayant m'attache à mon erreur.
> Et . . .
> Me dit que sans périr je ne me puis connaître. (II, 1)

> I do not know who I am; and to crown the horror, a terrifying oracle binds me to my error. And . . . tells me that I cannot know myself without perishing.

Born of a criminal union between Helen and Theseus, she lives under the pressure of wrongful concealment, feels the curse of the gods upon her, and cherishes a perverse and hopeless love for her enemy Achilles, in whose bloody arms she had once fainted. She revels in her misfortune as a pest that shall infect others, too, and becomes a spy and informer out of jealousy:

> Pour ne pas pleurer seule et mourir sans vengance. (II, 8)

In order not to weep alone and die without vengeance.

And she cloaks with convulsive shame all these seething passions, which do not escape Iphigénie's quiet glance:

Dieux qui voyez ma honte, où me dois-je cacher? (II, 8)

....

Souffrez que loin du camp et loin de votre vue
J'aille cacher un sort si digne de pitié,
Et dont mes pleurs encor vous taisent la moitié. (III, 4)

O gods who see my shame, where should I hide myself?

....

Far from the camp and far from your sight let me go hide a fate so worthy of pity, a fate only half revealed to you by my tears.

Having avenged herself, she ends by committing suicide. This means her penance, her salvation, and the saving of Iphigénie. This literary creation, relegated to a secondary role and used as a way out of an impossible situation, could only unfold timidly and in outline, as it were, within the framework of the pseudo-antique classical festival play. But it works on and grows in Racine's imagination, and ultimately steps into the daylight as Phèdre.[16]

PHÈDRE

The inspiration derived from Euripides and Seneca, the redolence of ancient classic literature and myths, in short, the humanistic feature, seems to be at least as persistent in *Phèdre* as in *Iphigénie*. In fact, it is essentially stronger in the former, because it has something more important to achieve than merely to serve as an ornament. In *Iphigénie* one cannot believe, even for the purposes of the stage, in the necessity of human sacrifice, in the revelations of Calchas, and in the power and greatness of the gods, when one sees and hears how those who are directly subject to them regard them as doubtful, when Agamemnon, in his distress of conscience, cries out,

Non, je ne croirai point, ô ciel, que ta justice
Approuve la fureur de ce noir sacrifice.
Tes oracles sans doute ont voulu m'éprouver;
Et tu me punirois si j'osois l'achever, (I, 1)

No, I will not believe, O heaven, that your justice approves the fury of this dark sacrifice. No doubt your oracles wanted to test me; and you would punish me if I dared to carry it out,

when he says of his own daughter:

Faites rougir ces dieux qui vous ont condamnée, (IV, 4)

Make those gods who condemned you blush,

when Clytemnestre objects,

Un oracle dit-il tout ce qu'il semble dire? (IV, 4)

Does an oracle say all it seems to say?

and when the whole world of the gods was only misunderstood.

It would be mistaken to condemn the gods in *Iphigénie* as a mere external arrangement: for actually the oracle signifies a voice of conscience, but it is a confused and ambiguous voice. It sets the whole Greek camp in an uproar, throwing terror, dissension, anger, indignation, doubt and fear into all the worldly minds, and yet it only refers to Eriphile. In its deeper sense this drama of misunderstanding is a drama of the human conscience, but its ethical meaning is not brought out with full clarity here; one discovers it fully only in *Phèdre,* just as Eriphile, too, first finds her full meaning as a preliminary step toward Phèdre. Eriphile is the unknown guilty one on the Greek state ship which cannot stir as long as she is on board. But the connection between her crime and the Greek enterprise remains in the semidarkness of superstition, or rather it remains subject to the caprice of the gods. Nowhere do we long so much for light as in matters of conscience. This light is attained in *Phèdre*. Now the whole Greek mythology becomes the voice of conscience. There is hardly an antique ornament from which the eternal face of the moral law does not look out threateningly.

Jules Lemaître has portrayed this relationship so gracefully that it would really be a pity not to let him speak for himself:

This Christian Phèdre of the seventeenth century and of the present day is the daughter of Minos and Pasiphaé and granddaughter of the Sun God; the coquettish, gay, clever, and shrewd Aricie, who allows herself to be seduced by Hippolyte only when she has the wedding ring on her finger, is the world's great-granddaughter. And both name their ancestors as if it were the most natural thing to do. We hear of Scirron, of Procuste, of Sinnis, and of the Minotaur. We learn that one fine day Phèdre's husband climbed down into the Tartarus to *déshonorer la couche* [dishonor the bed] of Pluto. We are in a world in which the gods hold monsters at the disposal of their favorites, in which the sea spits out giant snakes with the heads of bulls. Verses occur in which the people who just now seemed quite close to us suddenly reveal themselves as people of the most remote antiquity, when the great convulsions of nature still tremble, and long extinct species of animals may perhaps have lived—the days of the first human colonies, of the monsters and the heroes. The thrilling drama, that could just as well be of today, carries along in its wake fragments of myths thirty and forty centuries old . . . a bewildering effect, one might think. Yet that is not so. I shall cite only one place where age-old myth and highly modern drama mingle and fuse harmoniously in the intuitive vision of a sensitive hearer. Phèdre says:

Misérable! et je vis, et je soutiens la vue
De ce sacré soleil dont je suis descendue?
J'ai pour aieul le père et le maître des Dieux;
Le ciel, tout l'univers est plein de mes aïeux.
Où me cacher? Fuyons dans la nuit infernale.
Mais que dis-je? Mon père y tient l'urne fatale. . . . (IV, 6)

Wretch! And I live and bear the sight of that sacred sun from which I am descended? My forefather is the father and the master of the gods; heaven, the entire universe, is thronged with my ancestors. Where can I hide? Let us fly to the infernal night. But what am I saying? My father keeps the fatal urn there . . . .

In the most painful moment of the action Phèdre reminds us that Zeus is her earliest ancestor, Helios her ancestor, and Minos her father. This family tree withdraws her from us by some three thousand years, and this just at the moment when we have the most heartful longing to feel her close to us. Must not this mythologism make for disillusionment? By no means, for immediately afterward it changes; and Zeus, and Helios, and the cosmos, filled with the ancestors of this sinner, awaken in us the thought of the omnipresent eye of God, as it shines into our own conscience from everywhere. Minos is the eternal judge, before whom the soul must appear after death; and if Phèdre, broken by fear, falls on her knees and cries for forgiveness, she may be beseeching it of Minos, but we understand, nevertheless, that it is Racine's God who is meant.[17]

These tremors of conscience even vibrate through the story of Hippolyte's death, that magnificent piece that would have remained an academic imitation of the reports of the messengers in Euripides and Seneca if Racine had not electrified all the characters of his play with the consciousness of guilt. Phèdre's anguish of soul creeps through the hearts of those around her like a contagious fever, and scarcely one of them is spared by it. Even Oenone, the conscienceless old woman, is convulsed with it: "*Je l'ai bein mérité*!" (I have well deserved it!) she cries, and throws herself into the sea. The resolute Thésée, whose love of pleasure and eagerness to accomplish great feats have never been hindered by any reflection, loses his manly gaiety:

> Et moi-même, éprouvant la terreur que j'inspire,
> Je voudrois être encore dans les prisons d'Epire . . . . (III, 5)
> . . . .
> Ai-je pu mettre au jour un enfant si coupable? (IV, 3)
> . . . .
> Mais moi-même, malgré ma sévère rigueur,
> Quelle plaintive voix crie au fond de mon coeur? (V, 4)

> And I myself, feeling the terror I inspire, would like to still be in the prisons of Epirus. . . .
> . . . .
> Could I have sired so guilty a child?
> . . . .

But myself, in spite of my severe rigor, what plaintive voice cries from the bottom of my heart?

Finally his pangs of conscience grip him to such an extent that all his renown and the favor of the gods become a curse to him.

De l'univers entier je voudrois me bannir.
Tout semble s'élever contre mon injustice.
L'éclat de mon nom même augmente mon supplice.
Moins connu des mortels, je me cacherois mieux.
Je hais jusques au soin dont m'honorent les Dieux;
Et je m'en vais pleurer leurs faveurs meutrières. (V, 7)

I would like to banish myself from the entire universe. Everything revolts against my injustice. The very luster of my name increases my torture. If I were less known to men I could hide myself better. I hate the very attentions with which the gods have honored me; I go now to bemoan their baneful favors.

"To expiate" is his last thought. The slayer of dragons, accustomed to victory, ends up as a penitent. His innocent son, Hippolyte, the natural young man, feels poisoned and sickened. His pure love for Aricie seems to him something of a mistake, a kind of self-alienation:

Par quel trouble me vois-je emporte loin de moi?
. . . .
Maintenant je me cherche et je ne me trouve plus. (II, 2)

What anguish carries me far from myself?
. . . .
Now I seek but can no longer find myself.

After Phèdre has permitted him to look into her heart, he feels himself to be defiled:

Je ne puis sans horreur me regarder moi-même. (II, 6)
. . . .
Quel funeste poison
L'amour a répandu sur toute sa maison! (III, 6)

> Even I can no longer see myself without horror.
> . . . .
> What a pernicious poison love has spread over his entire household.

If he is unable to justify himself successfully before Thésée, this is because in his heart he can no longer feel that he is quite pure. True, he asserts:

> Le jour n'est pas plus pur que le fond de mon coeur, (IV, 2)

> Daylight is not purer than the depths of my heart,

and as regards the suspicion concerning Phèdre, if he speaks the truth, if he were as sure of himself as he is of her, he would express himself more calmly, and there would be no need of any "*affreux serment*" (frightful oath). Does not a faint shadow of pharisaism—one might say Jesuitism when one thinks of Racine and Port Royal—pass through the soul of this youth, who entrusts his cause solely to the just judgment of the gods?

> Sur l'équité des Dieux osons nous confier:
> Ils ont trop d'intérêt à me justifier;
> Et Phèdre, tôt ou tard de son crime punie,
> N'en sauroit éviter la juste ignominie. (V, 1)

> Let us put our faith in the justice of the gods. It is in their interests to justify me. Sooner or later, Phèdre, punished for her crime, will be unable to avoid just ignominy.

And if his young heart were not disturbed and frightened, would he have needed such an excessive and fearsome array of sacred assurances before he could marry his Aricie? It is not in order to make him a gallant character, but to show him as uncertain, to shake his conscience, that Racine represents his Hippolyte as being in Love: "I call weakness the passion that he feels, in spite of himself, for Aricie, who is the daughter and sister of his father's mortal enemies."

Théramène, the genial tutor of the young man, definitely thinks otherwise; for him there is nothing sinister, nothing of original sin, in love.

Enfin, d'un chaste amour pourquoi vous effrayer?
S'il a quelque douceur, n'osez vous l'essayer?
En croirez-vous toujours un farouche scrupule?
Craint-on de s'égarer sur les traces d'Hercule? (I, 1)

After all, why take fright at a chaste love? If there is sweetness in it why not dare to try it? Will you always cling to such fierce scruples? Can one go wrong following in the footsteps of Hercules?

And so on. And it would be just this levelheaded man of the world, with his sound and banal common sense, who has to look on at his pupil's frightful end. What his own dread does not tell him, springs to his senses as a howling monster of the deep. Of all this he can grasp only the horror and the horribleness.

Aricie is stricken by misfortune, it is true, but she is untouched by any poison of the soul. It is only her healthy warm heartedness and freshness that succeed in withstanding the infection that emanates from Phèdre. Without brooding, she always finds the right word, and always knows when to remain silent. Blessed with feminine genius of the heart, she walks through a pestilential world which, though it can take everything from her, really cannot get at her. She wishes to be banished from good society because she is born for marital love and domesticity:

Hélas! qu'un tel exil, Seigneur, me seroit cher!
Dans quels ravissements, à votre sort liée,
Du reste des mortels je vivrois oubliée! (V, 1)

Alas, my lord, how sweet such an exile would be to me! Linked to your fate, with what joy would I live forgotten by all other mortals!

As the only radiant figure, she stands on the edge of the drama, and her influence works inward toward its core, by her contrast to Phèdre.

Phèdre dominates and propels the whole, but not by the forcefulness of her action or of her self-determination. From the beginning she is lost, delivered up to her evil lust and her bad conscience. In her nature, heredity and thought work against one another, exciting and aggravating each other. Her love for Hippolyte is swollen, spiced, brought to the boiling point, dammed up by her awareness of its forbidden, shameful, dangerous, sinful nature, until its outbreak once more alerts the restraining forces, and the increased pressure heightens the explosive power. The forces of ancestry and of the reflecting mind, of sensuality and of conscience kindle each other and detonate as in a motor, consuming the physical and spiritual strength of this woman in their frantic, closed whirl. For she does not work outward; she has no vocation, no ability, and no desire to secure one for herself, and no intention of throwing off her misery. She is a mother and a queen, but for one smile from Hippolyte she would gladly throw away her child's birthright and her husband's throne. One can hardly imagine a less dramatic circumstance than this torture of a conscience in love with itself, and compounded of love, desire, greed, fear, and despair without an object. For it is all illusion. Hippolyte is the son of Thésée, not her son; hence the reproach of incest is untenable; her husband Thésée is believed dead, at least for a time, and there is no adultery involved, at the most a breach of good taste in prospect; but Hippolyte does not respond to her love, and so she would normally have to put the matter out of her head, especially since she has learned that the young man has another attachment. So she must surely be a fool, a psychopath?

Phèdre would lose her whole poetry and character were we to regard her through clinical eyes. Her essential being is spiritual and her illusion-fed mental conflict represents the ultimate wisdom and yearning of man.

Reines Herzens zu sein,
Das ist das Höchste,
Was Weise ersannen,
Weisere taten.

To be pure of heart,
That is the highest thing
That wise men have pondered about, and
Wiser men have achieved.

The sanest, the eternal, way and direction of our desire, the will to purify the heart, lives and works in Phèdre. Where this heavenly power takes hold of a person and all his roots, the ground must surely be torn up and everything around laid waste. The poet's task here was to make audible and visible this divine storm, this otherwordly hurricane that sweeps through the earthly tragedy. With the brilliant sobriety that distinguishes him, he has accomplished this task by making the inner soaring, the impetus of the heroine's spirit, appear as temporal laming, as frenzy and mental illness, and making the reeling giddiness of his Phèdre disquiet those around her and drive them to helping or hindering interventions that only delay and aggravate the misfortune but cannot eliminate it. And so there arises that heavenly yet demoniacal dual lighting, in which Phèdre steps forward, shown in all dimensions at once, as an impure, jealous, frightful, and, if you will, mentally sick creature, and as an angelically mild and pure being. Both views work together in such a way that, just as she is about to take the only really false step in her life, and admits her guilty love of Hippolyte, she finds the sweetest and noblest tones of the heart in which to do it. Never has a love believed to be criminal wheedled itself out in such innocent and tender words, only to show itself a few moments later as deadly frenzy (II, 5). The fear of hell and the yearning for heaven, balm and poison, mingle together in almost every one of her words.

In such a penetration of a tortured and a blessed, a cold and a devout vision of the world Racine's style achieves its highest peak. His interpreters are divided over whether to describe it as naturalistic or idealistic. It is not alternately, nor more or less, the one or the other, but always a unity of the two. The more passionately excited, distraught, and troubled in their minds Racine's characters are, the more restrainedly and clearly do they express themselves. They are not simply passion and nature, but rather the spirit of passion, the spirit of nature, spiritualized temperaments. On the other hand, the more restrained, quiet, cool, and enlightened, the more courtly, noble, and normal their bearing, the more warm, healthy, and robust is their feeling; for they are not stylized, conventional, or elegant in the usual sense. Rather are they nobility and gentility personified. Their apparent pose is warm-blooded refinement and wisdom of the heart. In *Phèdre* passion finds expression as intellect; in Aricie the normal healthy heart is expressed in tact and good manners. The tragedy in which they confront each other and clash is a paean to the omnipotence of conscience and the beauty of good behavior. Though the one stands in the way of and conflicts with the other in the action of the play, their reconciliation is effected at east in the artistic form, in the harmony and nobility of the work, its language and style. The ideal for which people suffer and die as for something unattained, is not placed in the other world; it is within the work, and reigns in it as perfected form:

> Wo sie sich zeige, sie herrscht, herrschet bloss, weil sie sich zeigt.

> Where she shows herself, she rules; she rules merely because she shows herself.

ESTHER

Esther and *Athalie* were written twelve and fourteen years respectively after *Phèdre* (1689 and 1691). They stand apart from Racine's secular dramas since they were meant for a special circle of spectators and were banned from the ordinary stage, and they deviate deliberately from the normal theatrical tradition. The scene of action is more mobile and open, the unity of time and place is lightly broken through, and lyrically elevated. With their choirs, songs, and musical accompaniment, they are akin to the modern opera and at the same time to the ancient Greek tragedies—Biblical and edifying, elegant and humanistic in tone. These loose and mixed forms may easily appear to be an alienation or turning away from the strictness of the classical style, if not actually a relapse into baroque, if one considers the technical exterior alone. On the other hand, they may be interpreted as a liberation of religious thought from the trammels of secular art and rules, if one emphasizes the particular character of the content, as Racine himself has done.

> Et vous, qui vous plaisez aux folles passions
> Qu'allument dans vos coeurs les vaines fictions,
> Profanes amateurs des spectacles frivoles,
> Dont l'oreille s'ennuie au son de mes paroles,
> Fuyez de mes plaisirs la sainte austérité.
> Tout respire ici Dieu, la paix, la vérité.
> (Prologue to *Esther*)

> And you who take pleasure in the mad passions with which pointless fictions inflame your hearts, you profane lovers of frivolous spectacles whose ears are bored by my words, flee from the holy austerity of my pleasures. All here breathes God, peace, and truth.

Instead of separating content and form, motive and technique, we should observe how they interpenetrate, for this is precisely where the secret of the work lies. Even the love tragedies, such as *Andromaque, Bérénice, Phèdre,* are no "*spectacles frivoles*" or "*vaines fictions.*" In their way they breathe the same "*sainte austérité*" as *Esther* and *Athalie,* and are in no way second to these in Christian sentiment and intellectual spirituality. It is only that they do not specifically name the God of Holy Scripture and the Church, and do not say "Lord, Lord" to him. It is essentially this explicitness of God's name that marks the contrast between the two "sacred" plays and the secular tragedies of our poet: not an external distinguishing mark, to be sure, but also not really non-essential. The main matter in question remains the same. One can describe it in Racine's own words as "*détachment du monde au milieu du monde même*" (detachment from the world in the midst of the world). It is Racine's old leitmotiv of renunciation, self-examination, conscience, merely transferred into a world in which this matter of the mind and heart is directly called God.

This God does not appear on the stage, but from it. He is constantly invoked, praised, revered, besought and—suffered. He appears directly only to the ear, not to the eye, the eye, that is, as inner countenance and hidden guide of the action, as the meaning of world events. The ear hears wonders; therefore the natural talk becomes intensified into song and takes refuge in music. The eye sees nothing but human action, though, to be sure, "*avec les seules scènes que Dieu lui-même, pour ainsi dire, a préparées*" (with isolated scenes that God himself, so to speak, has prepared; Preface to *Esther*); and for this reason the scene of action no longer remains as stationary and closed here as elsewhere, but vibrates or pulsates, so to speak—yet without ever forsaking the "Aristotelian" basis of unity of place and time, without overstepping the bounds of the human and natural.

A thrill of the divine throbs through the earthly happenings on the stage, as if the miraculous stood close behind the scenes, and shook them without venturing to come forward into the open. In *Esther* the humorous and in *Athalie* the uncanny and terrifying side of this state of things has been felt and indicated by the poet.

Something akin to the smiling magic of a fairy tale pervades *Esther*. The humorousness—if one could so describe the devout gaiety of a consummate man of the world, as Racine was—has two reasons, the practical one, namely the humorous subject, and then the fact that *Esther* was written for the aristocratic girls and young ladies of the school for daughters of the nobility at Saint-Cyr. Childish and virginal minds were to absorb, interpret, and present these compositions, and adult guests of high degree, including Louis XIV himself, were to be their delighted spectators. The play does not lose its meaning, it is true, but it does lose its peculiar charm, when we remove it mentally from this unique occasion, to which the prologue draws attention, as, with a few deft strokes of the pen, it sets the scene and the mood for us.

The Book of Esther, with its grim and evil story of lust, vengeance, and fanaticism, its Oriental splendor and odor of blood, becomes a fairy tale for the demoiselles of Saint-Cyr. The horrors are veiled or modified, the events telescoped, the circumstances childishly simplified, and the human and all too human motives traced back to God's direct decree. And all this, as Lotheissen says, "with a kind of artlessness that, when observed closely, is found to conceal a great art."[18] At times the literary expression overshoots the mark with well-weighed exaggeration and borders on expressionism—a very rare thing with Racine.

Dieu tient le coeur des rois entre ses mains puissantes;
Il fait que tout prospère aux âmes innocentes....

Un ange du Seigneur, sous son aile sacrée
A donc conduit vos pas et caché votre entrée?
Tout doit servir de proie aux tigres, aux vautours;
Et ce jour effroyable arrive dans dix jours.

Et la mort est le prix de tout audacieux...
Si le roi dans l'instant, pour sauver le coupable,
Ne lui donne à baiser son sceptre redoutable.

Sur ce trône sacré, qu'environne la foudre,
J'ai cru vous voir tout prêt à me réduire en poudre.

Peut-on, en le voyant, ne le connoître pas?
L'orgueil et le dédain sont peints sur son visage.

On lit dans ses regards sa fureur et sa rage.
Je croyais voir marcher la Mort devant ses pas....

Le sang de l'orphelin, les pleurs des misérables,
Sont ses mets les plus agréables.
C'est son breuvage le plus doux.

Au delà des temps et des âges,
Au delà de l'éternité!

God holds the hearts of kings between his powerful hands; he makes everything prosper for innocent souls....

Has an angel of the Lord covered your steps with his holy wing and hidden your entrance?

All must serve as prey to tigers, to vultures; and that terrible day is coming in ten days.

And death is the price of audacity...if the king, in order to save the guilty one, does not instantly give him his fierce scepter to kiss.

On this sacred throne surrounded by lightning I thought I saw you ready to reduce me to dust.

Can one on seeing him not know him? Pride and contempt are painted on his face.

His fury and his rage can be read in his looks. I thought I saw death walking before him....

The blood of orphans, the tears of the wretched, are his most agreeable dishes. It is his sweetest drink.

Beyond time and the ages, *beyond eternity*!

The ancient language of the Bible and the psalms, with its primitive starkness, is adapted into a language suitable for the young. Similarly, the simplicity and seriousness of the robust psychology and character-drawing of the Semitic original is retained, but placed in a light suitable for children's eyes. Thus Aman is made a proud and wicked man who cannot tolerate the fact that the Jew Mardochai will not salute him, the highest dignitary in the land. So he gives orders for the whole Jewish race to be exterminated. The decisive change in the heart of the Persian king comes about through a dream.

Motives and reasons such as these are not false; they have only been simplified and adapted to the faith of children. Assuerus is made like the king in a fairy tale—all-powerful, capricious, frightfully stern, magnificent, and very dangerous, but nevertheless good and just. He only has to be enlightened, and manipulated shrewdly, in order that his strong, punitive arm shall not strike the innocent. Esther is courageous, self-sacrificing, fearless in face of death, and at the same time very clever and cautious, in fact cunning, but nevertheless without falsehood. There is no harm at all in her marrying a despotic pagan king, hiding her racial origin from him, and wielding her feminine charms for the good of her own people. Why should not the end justify the means just a little bit here, where God's will is so manifest, and those on His side are good in every way, whereas those against Him are thoroughgoing scoundrels? What would be impure in the light of reality is pure and natural in the light of faith. The action of the play takes place in a world in which the great strivings and struggles of state and politics take on the appearance of a fairy tale for children.

To be sure, this naïveté is somewhat self-conscious, and does not appear devoid of coquetry on the stage. More especially, the choir of Jewish maidens, when it appears outside of the plot and addresses the stalls occupied by the gentlemen of the court, gives a painful impression of consciously graceful charm and beautiful sentiments.

> Foibles agneaux livrés à des loups furieux,
> Nos soupirs sont nos seules armes....
>
> Je tomberai comme une fleur
> Qui n'a vu qu'une aurore.
> Hélas! si jeune encore....

Weak lambs delivered over to furious wolves, our sighs are our only arms....

I will fall like a flower that has seen only a single dawn. Alas! still so young....

The sweet, innocent little doves! It was not the wickedness of the world alone that made performances of *Esther* become more and more a tidbit for elderly gourmets.

Yet not even the all too French charm, nor the praises of the king and of Madame de Maintenon with which the drama is sown, have injured its objective seriousness and dignity. True, of its inmost nature—that is to say, in its inspiration, and not merely because of the occasion that elicited it—it is and remains an incidental piece of literature; but the courtier's work of homage unfolds as a garland of human piety. Suprasensual thought expresses itself best in lyric poetry. Since the drama had been circumscribed on every side—anchored on the words of the Bible, decided and put in motion by God's decree, approved for the stage by the king's mistress—Racine's poetical individuality could only express itself fully in the interludes of the play, and brighten up the stony landscape with lyrical flowers wherever a little space was left. These lyrical flowers consist mainly of the choral songs, but they also fill a number of pauses in the action, for instance, Esther's famous monologue in the first act,[19] and the part songs or duets, expressing reflection, remembrance, fear, and hope, that occur in every scene. These are also expressive of the surging emotion of spirits moved by the hand of God, a mysterious condition from which not a single character in the Biblical play can escape, but to which none bow so directly and willingly, for none experience, cherish, and feel so consciously within themselves as the choir of Jewish maidens. They are part of the action because their weal or woe depends on it, for they are Esther's companions and spiritual sisters. But they are also outside of the action because they can take no hand in the course of things and must leave everything in the hands of the Lord their God. Their wisdom is the simple and universal wisdom of religion as a feeling of dependence on the heavenly powers, and could be clothed in pagan just as well as in Jewish terms.

The form of expression of the Hebrew psalms lends itself effortlessly to the classical Greek chorus. In the process the rugged genius of the ancient Biblical expressions is toned down and moderated to girlish sweetness. The content of thought, even the very letter of the psalms, remains, but the intonation, the sounds, and the rhythm are new. Compare, for instance, Psalm 36, verses 35 ff.:

Vidi impium superexaltatum et elevatum sicut cedros Libani: et transivi, et ecce non erat: et quaesivi eum, et non est inventus locus ejus.

and:

J'ai vu l'impie adoré sur la terre,
Pareil au cèdre, il cachoit dans les cieux
  Son front audacieux.

Il sembloit à son gré gouverner le tonnerre,
  Fouloit aux pieds ses ennemis vaincus.
Je n'ai fait que passer, il n'étoit déjà plus. (III, 9)

I have seen the impious one adored on earth. Like a cedar he hides his bold brow in the heavens.

He seems to govern the thunder as he will, he treads his vanquished enemies beneath his feet. I merely passed, and he was already gone.

Has not Racine laid a certain *esprit de finesse*, a positively feminine pleasantness and a gracefully clever irony, over the rugged words of the Psalmist?

The alternately light and heavy surge and swell of human souls under the wind of the spirit of God pulsates through the whole drama. In the choral songs it surges up into music, and in the recitatives, dialogues, and part songs it fades away to a faint whisper or a dull murmur. In this way the prescribed framework of the plot is inundated and enlivened with lyric poetry—poetry such as Racine had always used, but which up till then had remained caught up in the dramatic action in somewhat the same way that the music of an orchestra is led by the movements of the conductor's hands and arms, and is produced by visible stringed, wind, and percussion instruments—in short, by action. Here, on the contrary, music is produced in the trap of the theater, with an invisible conductor and musicians who do not see the action, and the ear can linger, completely absorbed in the purity of the sound. *Esther* is a work composed of colorful songs and shadowy drama.

ATHALIE

Though the occasion, the commission, and the public were the same, and the stage conditions were also similar, *Athalie* turned out completely different from *Esther*. "This time," says Paul Mesnard, "Racine's genius led him to heights of which those who had commissioned this second play had no inkling; he seemed to forget completely both the stage and the performers for whom he was working."[20] He forgot them because it had become natural to him to believe that God's providence can accomplish, in the most restricted space and with the feeblest instruments, a judgment that determines the face of mankind and the face of the earth for millennia to come. The sublimity of this composition rests on the contrasting interplay of earthly and heavenly dimensions and values. Viewed with the eyes of experience, it nowhere oversteps the scope of the stage nor the possibilities of production, but the convulsions and the universal visions it releases mock the boards of any theater. It does not burst through, but rather transcends the form of the drama; and indeed actually enclosed and rounded off in this form, in sense and meaning the play goes far beyond the form.

Only the real facts are dramatic, that is to say, brought about by human desires and actions; but events slip past the hero and draw him away into epic space and prophetic distance. This over-life-size and distant effect may well be present in almost every drama that has real meaning. But the particular additional circumstance here is that the persons in question feel and know themselves to be the instruments, vessels, victims, or media of higher powers to a degree hardly compatible with human free will. Nearly all of them have a second face, whether as presentiment *within themselves* or as appearance *of themselves*. This does not make them wooden, or unauthentic, or nondramatic. But they take on epic proportions, like statues, monuments, or colossal figures of themselves, and their voices range over the centuries. One would feel inclined to despair of finding actors capable of such pathos combined with such spiritual stature. For it is precisely through their spirituality that these characters have such a powerful effect. Their greatness does not depend on exaggeration but rather on restraint and austerity, and it cannot effectively be rendered visible by expressionistic means. This spirituality does not represent itself, therefore there is nothing symbolical about it; it appears as essential nature and intellectuality, and works, if I may say so, phenomenologically. Joad, Athalie, Mathan, and the rest are phenomena of human personality and spiritualized natures, not symbolical or mythical figures, allegorical spirits, or models and examples.

We must examine the dual lighting by which such phenomenology comes into being.

To the perceptive reader the high priest Joad must appear on the one hand as a desperately brave, resolute champion of the faith and prophet of God, and on the other, as a narrow-minded fanatic, a crafty politican, and a quarrelsome priest. He has a great or a cold heart, a broad or a puny mind, a far-seeing or a time-serving outlook, an authentic or a false soul, according to how you look at him. In one passage Racine himself appears to have become uncertain about this contradictory being. This one gathers, not of course from the drama itself, but from his supplementary "Remarques sur Athalie."[21] We know this from the second scene of Act V, because Racine has collected examples and texts from the Bible and the Fathers of the Church to justify the deception which Joad practices on Athalie with the Temple treasures, by which he lures her into the heavily fortified house of God as into a trap. There is not the least doubt that the poet deliberately gives Joad the detestable quality of dual morality. For after all, does he not put into his mouth such expressions as "*heureux larcin*" (happy theft; I, 2), "*saintes cohortes*" (holy cohorts; III, 7), "*Dieu dont l'intérêt me guide*" (God whose interest guides me; IV, 3), "*dans l'infidèle sang baignez-vous sans horreur*" (bathe without horror in the blood of infidels; IV, 3), "*ces fameux lévites qui...de leurs chers parents saintement homicides, consacrérent leurs mains dans le sang des perfides*" (these famous Levites who...piously homicidal by birth, consecrate their hands in the blood of the infidel; IV, 3), "*Grand Dieu, voici ton heure, on t'amène ta proie*" (Great God, this is your hour, we bring you your prey; V, 3), "*L'ange exterminateur est debout avec nous*" (the exterminating angel is standing by our side; V, 4), and so on.

The utterances of this inflexible theocrat and God-fearing slaughterer of men simply drip with blood and vengeance, humility and love, from his forked tongue. We would be very much mistaken were we to regard him as a hero after Racine's own heart. But neither does the poet attempt to belittle, suspect, or disapprove of him. There can be no question of either liking or disliking in face of such a pure phenomenon as he.

In *Athalie,* too, it is only the phenomenon—the alternating light and shade, the conflict of heavenly and earthly forces for possession of her—that arouses the poet's imagination, not her human or spiritual value. She herself is not anxious even about the salvation of her own soul, so tortured is she by pangs of conscience, forebodings, dreams, motherly feelings, and desire for domination. Like Joad, she has her responsibility, her ethical center of gravity, outside of herself; and since she cannot find it in God, she throws it into enmity toward Him.

> Impitoyable Dieu, toi seul as tout conduit.
> C'est toi qui me flattant d'une vengeance aisée,
> M'as vingt fois en un jour à moi-même opposèe,
> Tantôt pour un enfant excitant mes remords,
> Tantôt m'éblouissant de tes riches trésors. (V, 6)

> Pitiless God, you alone have done this. It is you who, flattering me with hope of an easy vengeance, twenty times in a day set me against myself, sometimes exciting my remorse because of a child, sometimes dazzling me with your rich treasures.

Comforted by the prospect that the game would go on and was bound to bring the God of the Jews many a defeat, she gives up her position—not her cause—as lost, and goes to her death.

> Que dis-je souhaiter? je me flatte, j'espère
> Qu'indocile à ton joug, fatigué de ta loi,
> Fidèle au sang d'Achab, qu'il a reçu de moi,
> Conforme à son aïeul, à son père semblable,
> On verra de David l'héritier détestable
> Abolir tes honneurs, profaner ton autel,
> Et venger Athalie, Achab et Jézabel. (V, 6)

> Why do I say I "wish"? I feel sure, I trust, that rebellious to your yoke, weary of your law, faithful to the blood of Achab, which he has received through me just like his father and grandsire the detestable heir of David will abolish your honors, profane your altar, and avenge Athalie, Achab, and Jézabel.

Her heroic freethinking appeals, like every religion, to the future.

Moral self-alienation on religious grounds reaches its height in the figure of the apostate Mathan, who goes over to Baal from Jehovah out of sheer ambition for high office. For Mathan is driven to despair because he cannot cease to believe in the God whom he has betrayed. The metaphysical contradiction in which he finds himself, puts his conscience into a frantic state and makes him completely shameless. If he had a less religious nature this kind of severance of all human consideration, all natural decency and sense of shame, would hardly have taken place in him. The third scene of Act III, in which he discards his last pretense, seems crass and painful, but we should not carp at it as improbable or untrue. That it is no longer *dans la nature,* as Houdar de la Motte says, may be admitted. Metaphysical eruptions are never *dans la nature.* Mathan knows this better than do his oversqueamish and socially well-brought-up critics.

Du Dieu que j'ai quitté l'importune mémoire
Jette encore dans mon âme un reste de terreur;
Et c'est ce qui redouble et nourrit ma fureur.
Heureux si...
Je puis...
A force d'attentats perdre tous mes remords! (III, 3)

The importunate memory of God, whom I have abandoned, thrusts into my soul a remnant of terror; and this it is that doubles and nourishes my fury. Happy if... I can... after many attempts conquer all remorse.

The child Joas, on whom the expectations, hopes, and fears of both parties are centred, and upon whose head the blood-stained crown of David comes to rest, is a piously brought up, innocent creature, and knows nothing of either good or evil except from hearsay. His candor, intelligence, and serenity, the inexpressible charm of his nature, stem less from purity of heart than from ignorance of all temptation and danger. There is something at once supernatural and indoctrinated about his alertness of mind, something of the child prodigy and of the parrot. With one glance Athalie sizes up the drill and polish, and senses behind it a kindred worm-eaten heart in which a tyrant and murderer lies latent, and where her own wild blood still circulates peacefully and yet unsuspectingly.

Enfin, Éliacin, vous avez su me plaire;
Vous n'êtes point sans doute un enfant ordinaire. (II, 7)

Eliacin, you have finally been able to please me. You are doubtless not an ordinary child.

This nine-year-old with the double name Eliacin-Joas has a Janus head. While his face is still that of a child, people delight in him and take care of him, almost as the good Josabet, his foster mother, does. But all this amiability fades away as if at the wave of a magic wand as soon as we see the averted criminal face mirrored in the prophetic glance of his tutor:

Comment en un plomb vil l'or pur s'est-il changé? (III, 7)

How has pure gold changed into vile lead?

Among the leading and decisive personalities in the plot of the play, there is not one that can hold our human sympathy, not one from whom it does not have to turn away in a decisive moment, not one whose statuesque proportion is proof against the shrinkage to which all temporal things are subject. In regard to these heroic figures we experience something like what Athalie sees in her mother in a dream:

Ma mère Jézabel devant moi s'est montrée,
Comme au jour de sa mort pompeusement parée...
Et moi, je lui tendois les mains pour l'embrasser.
Mais je n'ai plus trouvé qu'un horrible mélange
D'os et de chair meurtris, et trainés dans la fange.... (II, 5)

Jézabel, my mother, showed herself to me, richly adorned as on the day of her death... and I, I put out my hands to embrace her. But I found only a terrible mixture of bones and flesh, bruised and dragged in the mud....

Only the secondary figures—Abner, Josabet, Zacharie, Salomith, the chorus, the priests, the Levites, the confidants and so on—remain to some degree like themselves and stand more or less outside the historical and religious viewpoint, which magnifies or minimizes, ennobles or debases, everything that it fastens on. But even these, who only perform subsidiary services and are small advancers of great happenings, and so may keep their natural human ways, are made foolish and foppish, at least exteriorly, and seem almost comical figures. It is not an emphatic and conscious comicality, however, but rather extrinsic and involuntary when, for instance, Abner, the brave soldier, arrives too late to take part in the siege of the Jewisch prophets' party. The high priest knows that an officer of such strict ideas of honor and conscience dare not be initiated into the secrets of theocratic politics. And the queen knows that when it comes to conflicts between church and state, he must be chained up.

> Je sais que dès l'enfance élévé dans les armes
> Abner a le coeur noble, et qu'il rend à la fois
> Ce qu'il doit à son Dieu, ce qu'il doit à ses rois. (II. 4)

> I know that trained to arms since childhood Abner has a noble heart, and that he renders both what he owes his God and what he owes his kings.

That good creature Josabet is continually driven by her anxieties and fears to give advice and express opinions that, viewed in the light of the divinely ordained course of history, are petty and definitely wrong every time. To be too conscious of being in God's hands is very unpleasant to her.

> Dieu défend-il tout soin et toute prévoyance?
> Ne l'offense-t-on point par trop de confiance? (III, 6)

> Does God prohibit all care and all caution? Doesn't one offend him by too much confidence?

Zacharie is a dear, pompous little creature, a newsmonger and a hothead, a mediocre and feeble imitation of his father.

True, Salomith and the choir of Jewish maidens take part in the dramatic action on the side of the prophets' party against the queen, offer their services, and accompany the action. But in reality they are able to give voice only to their human and feminine distress and perplexity in face of the struggle for power, and to put questions this way and that, torn as they are between the will of God and the decisions of men.

Que de craintes, mes soeurs, que de troubles mortels!...
Quel spectacle à nos yeux timides! (III, 8)
....
Quel est ce glaive enfin qui marche devant eux? (IV, 1)

How many fears, my sisters, how much mortal anguish!. . .
What a spectacle for our timid eyes!
....
What, then, is this sword that goes before them?

The half-light in which the choir feels and seeks its way represents the spiritual and lyrical frame of mind that gives rise to the prophecy of Joas.

Que du Seigneur la voix se fasse entendre,
Et qu'à nos coeurs son oracle divin
  Soit ce qu'à l'herbe tendre
Est, au printemps, la fraîcheur du matin. (III, 7)

May the Lord's voice be heard, and may his divine oracle be to our hearts what the tender grass is, in the spring, the freshness of morning.

But after hearing the revelation, they are no wiser than before.

Le Seigner a daigné parler.
Mais ce qu'à son prophète il vient de révéler,
Qui pourra nous le faire entendre?
S'arme-t-il pour nous défendre?
S'arme-t-il pour nous accabler? (III, 8)

The Lord has deigned to speak. But who can make us hear what he has just revealed to his prophet. Does he arm himself to defend us? Does he arm himself to overwhelm us?

That is what the poet wanted. "One may add that this prophecy serves greatly to increase the trouble in the play by the consternation and the different movements into which it throws the chorus and the principal actors" (Preface).

"*Trouble et consternation*"—perplexity and dismay—do in fact dominate the whole course of events. And those concerned, even the most self-possessed heroes, only guess but do not understand its import, for "history is of God's making," and the things that happen in *Athalie,* the action that, according to the letter, in concentrated in the hall of the priests' house in the Temple of Jerusalem, is, in its inmost meaning, the prelude to the mightiest event in human history. For these things are the tremendous labor and pangs, so to speak, that herald the breakdown of the Old Covenant and that clear the way for the birth of Christianity.

> Peuples de la terre, chantez.
> Jérusalem renaît plus charmante et plus belle. (III, 7)
>
> Peoples of the earth, sing. Jerusalem is reborn more enchanting and more beautiful.

Is it any wonder that, against such a background, the human and individual elements of the stage play show up pale, and the dramatic gestures give way and become relatively unimportant under the impact of the exalted and solemn words? We know that in the French theater society with its system of confidants, its courtly gallantry, its manners, customs, rules of etiquette, titles, and so forth, played a more or less comparable role, and stood for a concept similar, to that of fate in Greek tragedy. In *Athalie* these social forms are reduced to a trifling remnant and have had to give way to the *modern* fate, which is called politics and world history.

According to the Jewish and the Christian way of thinking, which dominated Racine, politics and history really signify God's action on earth. And in order to express our poet's attitude, we may use the words of an important religious thinker and philosopher of today: "Racial and tribal history (with which *Athalie* is as replete as is the Old Testament) is . . . the original soil on which the religious life is enacted; history in its beginnings is the ladder that draws together heaven and earth, the world and life. The religion of the civilized peoples really begins with history, in contrast to the religions that seem to us like mythology and always have the world as a material entity . . . for their object. Religion as the religion of the common people, of the masses, of mankind, of humanity, cannot cast aside its character as history."[22]

With the first words of his verse drama, Racine plunges us into this atmosphere of tribal history as the history of divine happenings in the world:

> Oui, je viens dans son temple adorer l'Eternel.
> Je viens, selon l'usage antique et solennel,
> Célébrer avec vous la fameuse journée
> Où sur le mont Sina la loi nous fut donnée . . .
>
> Yes, I come to adore the Eternal in his temple. I come, according to antique and solemn custom, to celebrate with you that wonderful day on which the law was given to us on Mount Sinai. . .

and it is only with the last verses that he dismisses us:

> Apprenez, roi des Juifs, et n'oubliez jamais,
> Que les rois dans le ciel ont un juge sévère,
> L'innocence un vengeur, et l'orphelin un père.
>
> Learn, king of the Jews, and never forget, that in heaven kings have a severe judge, innocence an avenger, and the orphan a father.

Breathing a sigh of relief, we step out of the oppressive atmosphere of theocracy and back into the natural existence that is tolerated there, perhaps also protected, but definitely not *recognized.*

Hence *Athalie* is an historical drama of politics and religion, where God and the king, ruling families and priestly dynasties, contend with each other. The smooth ground on which Racine's plays, like Molière's, usually run their course, namely, polite society—the educated private and court circles, the cultivated and civilized communication between man and man—is hardly capable of carrying the revolutionary upheavals and the giant personalities of this world court. As a work of art I would venture to compare *Athalie* with that metal colossus with feet of clay that Nebuchadnezzar saw in a dream and of which the prophet Daniel interpreted the meaning; his words are just as good a key to Racine's last and mightiest work as to the dream of the Babylonian king: "And as you saw the iron mixed with miry clay, so they will mix with one another in marriage; but they will not hold together, just as iron does not mix with clay."

Hence, one could describe *Athalie* in a term that Imbriani coined for Goethe's *Faust*, namely, an unsuccessful masterpiece, *un capolavoro sbagliato*,[23] the emphasis being assuredly on the word "masterpiece," the failure resting purely on the fact that the theatrical style of the time was not prepared and fortified for the power and force of this masterpiece. But let anyone to whom its inner and more sublime meaning really matters, hear how Daniel continues: "And in the days of those kings the God of heaven will set up a kingdom which shall never be destroyed, nor shall its sovereignty be left to another people. It shall break in pieces all these kingdoms and bring them to an end, and it shall stand for ever."

> Les rois des nations, devant toi prosternés,
> De tes pieds baisent la poussière . . .
> . . . .
> Et que la terre enfante son Sauveur.

> The kings of nations, prostrate before you, kiss the dust of your feet. . .
> . . . .
> And let the earth give birth to its Savior.

Les Cantiques Spirituels

With *Athalie* the literary composition had grown too grandiose for the stage, and as Racine had accustomed himself more and more to bringing his outward life into conformity with his spiritual life, he now renounced the theater. His most powerful work had not been given anything like a worthy production. The young ladies of Saint-Cyr were permitted to play it only in a locked hall and without costume. But even the most magnificent production imaginable would scarcely have satisfied the author.

Was it really the breadth and depth of the religious thought they contained that made *Esther* undramatic and *Athalie* unsuitable for the stage? It is precisely the religiousness of these pieces that such a perceptive critic as Mario Fubini disputes.

"In these works," he says, "in which great and somber pages of the Bible come alive, one seeks in vain the religious tones of mystery, fear, expectation, and horror in face of God's revelation. These two tragedies will never satisfy a strongly religious spirit. And in any case, who has ever read *Esther* and *Athalie* expecting to find in them a deeply religious spirit?"[24]

Certainly neither Racine nor his works is "religious" in the sense commonly understood today, that is, a hankering after ecstasies, twilit churches smelling of incense, and surges of soulful feelings. The romantic and theatrical is conspicuously lacking, precisely because it does not belong to the essential nature of religion at all, but is only a false manifestation of it. In Racine's work one never finds the religious beside the poetical, never as an addition or spicing, so to speak, never as the Turk who, as Hegel relates, wanted the painting of a fish. "The fish will accuse you on the Last Day for not having given him a soul."[25]

Certainly neither we nor Fubini would demand a special presentation and interpretation of the Biblical and religious in a Biblical and religious play. We would not, like Hegel's Turk, demand a definite representation of the soul of the fish alongside the fish. But the spirit of the theater, the French theater of that time, definitely demanded it. And that Racine himself expected something of the kind from himself is shown by his choruses, which he inserted as a kind of *cantiques spirituels*.

Later, after he had finally bidden farewell to the theater, he did in fact compose such canticles. But these, too, show once more how far from impassioned or extravagant, how austere and realistic, his spirtual writing is. It follows the Biblical text, and aims to adhere to it as closely as possible. It seeks its effectiveness and beauty, not in a free adaptation or paraphrase of the spiritual content, but in a devout devotion to it, in a heartfelt personal feeling for the Word of God. It adds nothing to it; it only smoothes and humanizes, for general consumption, that is, say, for the congregation of the faithful, the rugged wording of the original text.

En vain je parlerois le langage des anges;
  En vain, mon Dieu, de tes louanges
  Je remplirois tout l'univers:

Sans amour, ma gloire n'égale
Que la gloire de la cymbale
Qui d'un vain bruit frappe les airs.

I would, in vain, speak the language of the angels; vainly, my God, I would fill the entire universe with your praise; without love, my glory is only like that of a cymbal that beats the air with a vain noise.

The original text resounds in the memory; one must be initiated into this, one must know it and believe it, in order to appreciate the poetical character of such songs. They have this quality, not as something special in them but rather as something behind or above them that is natural and normal to the believer. Assuming devout faith in their hearers, they hark back to the object of this faith. One could say that it is an evocative and expressive poetry which, with a purely formal transparency, conveys familiar things to those already intimately acquainted with them. The simple intimacy of such songs requires no stage, no introduction, no opening other than open hearts. The same thing applies to *Esther* and *Athalie*. Their wealth of religious thought does not transcend the scope of the stage: its simple inwardness makes stage space superfluous.

4

Tragic Drama from Euripides to Racine

The theater tends to love material that is exotic and strange, that it can master and render spectacular and effective. And when Racine came on the scene, the French stage in particular was accustomed to the greatest possible contrast to the familiar, and the utmost strangeness and distance of subjects and characters. It delighted in presenting kings and princes of the remotest climes and times, curious complications, unusual conflicts, superhuman choices, and heroic decisions. The everyday was dismissed from the outset as undramatic, the familiar as banal and perhaps comical, the native and homely as lacking all attraction. All masters of the drama, particularly Corneille, strove after the exotic and the precious. In tragic drama nothing was more scorned than the adaptation and conforming of strange and ancient things and people to the native world of the present. Even sensible Boileau says:

> Gardez donc de donner, ainsi que dans Clélie,
> L'air ni l'ésprit françois à l'antique Italie;
> Et sous des noms romains faisant notre portrait,
> Peindre Caton galant et Brutus dameret.
> Dans un roman frivole aisément tout s'excuse...
> Mais la scène demande une exacte raison;
> L'étroite bienséance y doit être gardée.[1]

Do not then, as in Clélie, give the French air or spirit to classical Italy; and under Roman names make our portrait,

> paint Cato a gallant and Brutus a dandy. In a frivolous novel all is easily excused... but the stage demands exactitude, careful seemliness must be respected there.

A tragedy was hardly produced before people began anxiously investigating whether its Greeks, Romans, or Turks were genuine Greeks, Romans, and Turks and not perchance their own countrymen and contemporaries in disguise.

It would be mistaken to assume that this anxiety for so-called "historical truth" and "fidelity" was prompted by a genuine archaeological or academic interest. No, it was purely a question of *bienséance,* that is to say, of distance from reality not at all of consistence with it. The characters on the stage were meant to appear elegant, that is, far removed from the rough and tumble of the everyday, high above the atmosphere of the auditorium, and not familiar to anyone. The authenticity expected of them was not a matter of historical research, but of perspective and illusion. Hence Caesar appeared on the stage, not in a Roman toga, but in a French robe of state with a full-bottomed wig, and even Attila was obliged to lay aside his Hun's garb and don a court costume, as the taste of the time considered right and proper. A contemporary, not a historical, Caesar or Attila was presented by the actor playing the Caesar or the Attila of tragedy.

The same solemnity was expected in the speech of the actor playing a heroic role. Grandiloquent declamation, theatrical pathos, superhuman gravity and majesty were the rule.

Whence did this strange stylization derive? Definitely not from the medieval theatre. From the thirteenth century onward this had become more and more naturalistic. It was only with the Renaissance and the coming of humanism that the feeling for the purity and integrity of the tragic, as of the comic, as well as the demarcation of the high, medium, and lower styles, became sharpened.

Racine joined in this purification of public taste, and led his tragic style beyond that of his predecessors to the highest purity. He cast off the Baroque, precious, grotesque, naturalistic, or tragicomic influence that a Hardy, a Tristan l'Hermite, a Corneille, a Rotrou, and many others still adhered to, and thanks to his deepened humanistic education, he turned still further back past French, Italian, and Roman tragedy to the Greeks—to

Aeschylus, Sophocles, and Euripides. All these three he read thoroughly in the original texts. The remarks with which he covered his own copies permit us to follow the track of his observations to this day.[2]

A new spirit enveloped him when he stepped into this world; for generally speaking, people knew Greek tragedy only from Aristotle's *Poetics*[3] and from Roman and modern imitations. Moreover, people were accustomed to see and regard it as essentially a school study, hence as something prescribed, an exercise in art, or a system to value and use. To be sure, it was from their understanding of and sympathy with this world that the Italians' unexpected blossoming of melodrama and opera came. But for others, Greek drama remained dead, that is, a matter for the learned, the "*licenciados barbados,*" as Lope de Vega remarked contemptuously.[4]

It was reserved to Racine to discover in Greek tragedy something new, something, moreover, other than the spirit of the music and the chorus, something that I venture to call, with Boileau,

> Cette hauteur divine
> Où jamais n'atteignit la foiblesse latine.[5]
>
> That divine elevation never reached by Latin feebleness.

Nowhere in Racine does one find a conscious formula for this "divine sublimity," for he experienced it intuitively in his feelings and meditations rather than intellectually or concretely. To put it briefly, he was the first to see the tragic in Greek tragedy.

The lyrical, the musical, the solemn, the symmetrical, the literary power, the mythical, and, in a certain sense, religious nature of the matter had not escaped persons of classical education. But they simply had no eyes, and probably could have no eyes, for the core of classical tragedy, namely, its tragic nature. For neither medieval culture nor the humanistic Renaissance that followed it, had brought people up to the tragic view of life. "Tragedy" was to those ages partly a stylistic, partly a "raw material" concept, connected in their minds with a solemn art form and a terrifying or touching happening, not the experience of spiritual ruin.[6]

Real tragedy can be experienced only where otherwordly

forces grow so strong in the consciousness that they can destroy a human soul. Troubles and misfortunes that do not attack the soul, that do not rend and destroy it, can be considered tragic only in name and form, but not in meaning. That is why the Middle Ages, in so far as they were Christian and not, as in some instances, still pagan in thought, had no tragedy.

In its core the Catholic religion is not dualistic. In the whole body of medieval drama there is not a single play in which the devil is regarded and represented as the equal partner of God, or in which he does not have to play a secondary and, generally, even a ridiculous role as the defeated, the inferior in principle, in fact, the fooled and hoaxed character. The very names of these religious plays express their basically nontragic and confident character: *Mystére* from *ministerium,* with an occasional suggestion of *mysterium, devozione, sacra rappresentazione, auto sacramental,* all signify a holy action of which the ultimate aim and purpose is the redemption, the salvation of the soul, the happy ending, or as the Latin *ludus* indicates, the amusement of the faithful at the expense of Satan or Antichrist.

Even the death of Christ on the Cross was not taken tragically. The core of the Easter plays was the Resurrection, the *resurrectio,* not the *Passio.* The artistic problem of this theater was not the tragic conflict between God and the world but primarily the subjection of the world to God. Later, when this end had been ensured by the Church, the problem became more and more the technical question of how the liturgical and ecclesiastical character of the main plot could be reconciled with the secondary entertainment and the interludes, which were secular. The history of religious drama in the whole of the Western world shows a progressive theatricalizing of the sacramental, which ultimately resulted in a "de-divinization" and secularizing of the theater. Eventually it became mainly melodramatic and musical in Italy, nationalistic and martial in Spain, while in France it turned to allegorical and anecdotal didactics and entertainment. Everywhere the end product was a broad spectacle, which in compass and outlook could embrace the whole many-colored variety of world events. But for the tragedy of the soul, and for it alone, there was no place and no possibility among the many dreadful, coarse, wild, bloody, edifying, ridiculous, tender, and strange things portrayed.

The spell of unthinking sacramental faith, under which so

many devout persons live, even today, in spiritual complacency and security, could only be broken by a religious eruption and by philosophical thought. Luther, Calvin, Descartes, Pascal, and also the Spanish mystics, all gave the complacent, conformist Christian conscience a mighty shaking, unleashing spiritual anguish, storms, despair and illuminations in men's minds, drawing their thoughts inward, and thus making them alternately miserable and glorious in their own eyes. It was only when this inwardness, this pride and joy in and anxiety for his own spiritual strength, had been awakened in man that the whole tragic nature of human strivings and desires could be felt, seen, and portrayed dramatically.

The tragedy which Racine fashioned into words had first been lived by his fathers and mothers, sisters and brothers in Port-Royal. For Port-Royal was Racine's spiritual family, his real paternal home. That is why his work is so closely tied to Port-Royal in tone and spirit. Only as regards its form, not its experience and content, can it really be described as humanistic or even as literary. It is as if a son and brother were looking on at the sufferings and struggles of his family—inactive, it is true, in his fears and hopes for them, but moved all the more deeply by their sufferings, which he cannot avert; shattered by the conflict, in which he cannot intervene, bleeding from his own heart for the wounds of others, Racine experienced the tragedy of existence. This compassionate sympathy that *suffers* and bears in the *soul* what his family is suffering in the flesh, has the advantage of not being present otherwise than inwardly and spiritually, and so of allowing the poet to recognize and see the proximate sufferings of his own mirrored in all latitudes and in the most far-flung places—in Greece and Rome and Asia.

Racine read his Sophocles and Euripides with a conscience sharpened and rendered incorruptible by characters as deep and speakers as sincere and simple as Antoine Arnauld and Blaise Pascal. The men and women of Port-Royal, who had suffered and bled for their resistance to the politicizing of man's conscience, stood like elder brothers and sisters behind Racine, watching from above over the humanist and *litterateur*. They did not exercise an influence on him in the literary sense; on the contrary, they placed a hindrance and a shadow over him, protecting the religious and ethical spirit of Port-Royal against defilement by him through ancient and modern literature. Hence Racine saw in antique tragedy the eternal rather than the temporal, the content rather than the form.

In this he substantiated Pascal's great fundamental thought that the only religion that had existed from the beginning and would always exist is the Christian religion. "No sect or religion has been constantly on the earth except the Christian religion. The only religion against nature, against common sense, against our pleasures, is the only one that has always been."[7] Hence everything human must be related or referred to this natural and Christian universal religion, this timeless position of defense of the spirit against the flesh: "All conduct of anything must have for its object the establishment and the grandeur of religion; men must have in themselves sentiments that conform to what it teaches us; and finally it must be so much the object and center where everything tends, that whoever knows the principles can give satisfactory answers both for all of man's nature in particular, and for all undertakings of the world in general."[8]

I should have to quote two-thirds of Pascal's *Pensées* if I wished to establish the premises on which Racine's view of classical tragedy, in fact, his view of the whole past, rests so naturally that he was hardly conscious of it himself. Without knowing the *Formulations* in detail—they were only published in 1670, the year *Bérénice* was produced—and guided solely by the basic attitude of the men and women of Port Royal, Racine came to believe, know, and perceive that the doctrine of predestination, from which Christianity had renewed itself again and again, is in no wise a Pauline, Augustinian, Clavinistic, or Jansenistic Christian tenet, that it is not a discovery but a natural characteristic of all the deeper faiths, hence also of the Greek faith. The tragedy of predestination confronted him unmistakably, indeed imperatively, in Aeschylus, Sophocles, and Euripides; most openly, of course, in Euripides, as the most serious and sombre, the *τϱαγικοτατοσ* who knows, as none other does, how to conjure up on to the stage the *deus ex machina*, the incalculable god, and broken man. Racine's predilection for Euripides cannot be explained otherwise than in the light of Racine's preoccupation with the thought of predestination and that other concept so closely bound up with it, namely, man broken by original sin.

It may be that the Baroque taste for the ghastly, which found so much delight in Seneca's tragedies, also favored Euripides and commended him to our poet's attention. But a man versed in the whole of classical literature, a man of such independent mind as Racine, allows himself to be influenced by the trends and tastes of the day only in so far as these are favorable to his own inclination. To be sure, Racine found the cruel god with his caprices, his vengeance, and his favorites in the tragedies of Sophocles, too. But only Euripides could offer him what also belonged essentially to this concept of God for the pupil of the Jansenists—man inwardly uncertain, conscious of sin, weak, effeminate, at odds with himself.

When one sees him, only fifteen years old, reading his Plutarch with the thought of predestination and sin in his heart, and marking the Greek text with notes such as: "Grace—sufficient grace—*De libero arbitrio*—this is semi-Pelagian—Providence—Power of God—*Θεὸς μὲν αἰτἰαν φὖει Βροτοῖσ*. Gods authors of evil—Grace: men have no other sentiments than those which God gives them. *Ζεῦς δ' ἀρετὴν ἄνδρεττιν ὀφέλλει τε μινὺθει τε*—Grace—*ἑκάττῳ τι ἡμῶν κακὸν εττιν*: Original sin, etc."[9]—one can imagine how deeply imbued he was with religious determinism, and how attractive the ethical and metaphysical problems inherent in Euripides' works must have been to him. If he had considered the Greek tragic dramatists only with the humanist's feeling for beauty, and not with the eyes of his faith, there is no doubt that the more finished, tougher, and sterner art of Sophocles, which he knew very well, would have lured him away from Euripides and won him completely for itself. His almost artless predilection for Euripides proves that one cannot regard him as a *poeta philologus*, as Fubini is inclined to do—a kind of Politian, Vincenzo Monti, Platen, Carducci, or Leconte de Lisle—we must place him, rather, among the ethical and religious poets, the direct and great ones, as a spiritual brother of Dante, Milton, and Goethe. Not that we would wish to deny the humanistic, philological, scholarly, and aesthetic sides of his work. These are obvious, but they are not the essential, the original motive force. And did not Racine, the older he grew, despise and more and more avoid the beautiful and scholarly sides of humanistic literature?

It was not even the stage technique of Euripides that came alive for him; it was only his spiritual problems and his tragic muse. The *deus ex machina,* that most tangible expression of grace and of caprice—the alternating frightfulness and forgivingness of God—he avoids deliberately. The stage of his drama does not stem from Greek tragedy, nor indeed from antiquity at all, not even from Seneca, whom he likewise knew and often used.

As stage plays Racine's tragedies are essentially nonantique, however unambiguously they observe, according to the letter, the Aristotelian unities of time and place. The theater of antiquity was meant to represent a firm square which the god Dionysus protected, consecrated, and used in order to give men a spectacle to watch as his guests and spectators. The oldest tragedies were presented within the precincts of the Eleuthereus of Dionysus,[10] and one must think of the theater as being in the vicinity of the temple, the dwelling of the godhead. To the Greek mind the godhead was much more closely and directly bound to certain holy places than in the Jewish and Christian minds. This is probably mainly accountable for the fact that the Greek stage held so firmly to the unity of a certain place.

The play is not meant to overstep the favorite haunt of the god, who is thought of as being present there, and is represented by a statue. Dionysus is doubtless mobile and able to wander through every land, but he stands as divine producer before the spectacle around which his *δέμοσ*, his believers, are assembled, and by his silent presence protects the place into which the chorus and the drama are led; *εἰσάγειν δρᾶμα* is the technical expression. Such a tragedy was officially opened with the words "Aeschylus, lead in the chorus!" and the actors followed the chorus into the consecrated place. And even if things happened which "did not concern Dionysus," as the saying was, nevertheless, thanks to this introduction, they were still steeped in *his* air, in the tragic space that was *his*. The stage of Dionysus acquired the spiritual value of the integrally tragic, and continued to exist as a religious framework even when the aesthetic or imaginary space was transferred to the province of other gods, or even into other lands. Wherever the piece was played, it counted as played in the home of Dionysus. He stood before it and was active in it as the Naiads were active in the healing fountain, that is, in an effective and magical way, and not, say, only as spectators.

The purification of the human spirit by tragedy, the catharsis so famed since Aristotle, can hardly have been other, in its original sense, than a healing action emanating from Dionysus, a magic by which he thrilled and strengthened the faithful at the Dionysia, his festival plays. His healing action was, like that of a health resort, bound in place and time to the Dionysia. And if the art of the tragic drama produced an alibi and moved the spectator from Athens to, say, Aulis, it remained with Dionysus in effect and inner meaning. The chorus, to which the drama hung as a fluttering flag hangs to a flagstaff, guaranteed this union, this effective meaning. The idea of an arbitrary leap through space and time within the drama, the modern manipulation of stage wings and scenerery, can only take place where the drama is *produced*, not *introduced*, where it brings its own space with it and carries it in a trunk for free disposal, as a wandering player carries his costume.

The Christian drama of the Middle Ages did not have any changes of scene either as long as its aesthetic room was enclosed in the mystical and religious room of the Church, and it was played in the house of God or at least in its vicinity. But from the beginning the Christian plays stood in an essentially different relation to their God from the Greek ones. They were performed in God's honor and under His eye, but not under His divine and healing action. They were never regarded as sacraments, nor as actual mysteries, but only as embellishments of the divine services. Only an edifying, instructive, and entertaining function was ascribed to them, never a purifying one. The Redemption was represented and glorified in them, but not consummated; for after all it had been achieved, concluded, and authenticated by the Resurrection and by the existence of the Church.

Since the Redemption of mankind was inherent as motive in medieval drama but only implicitly present as dogmatic subject, the stage of the medieval play had to be the whole religious universe, heaven, earth, and hell, embracing the whole of man's earthly life from the Creation to the Last Judgment, capable of extending from Jerusalem to Rome, Constantinople, St. James of Compostella, and so on, and had to move around amid all the scenes and times of divine action and human activities, all of which could only be achieved symbolically and by implication. This overworld and world stage was a great *machina ex Deo*, that is to say, according to the spirit of the thing, a divine apparatus, but according to objective fact, a wooden contraption. From the twelfth to the sixteenth century the problem of how far the sacred, ecclesiastical, eternal meaning of the happenings on this stage were reconcilable with the secular, temporal, natural, and anecdotal scenes portrayed, was under perpetual discussion.

Various ways were tried with a view to overcoming this artistic problem of portraying the human world in the bosom of the divine one, but they all ended in secularization and naturalism. The overshadowing religious compass of time and world space fell away or evaporated. The separate scenes of the drama became free, mobile, and transferable within an expanse of time and space emptied of the divine, from which the various excerpts could be taken at will.

About the year 1600 the theaters of Europe offered a wide variety of scenic possibilities which I do not propose to describe in detail here.[11] There was no extension, no consecutive order, no box set, no transformations, no alternating scenes of action, no overcutting, shortening, or lengthening of time, no switching back and forth in the course of the action that was not tried and carried out, nothing that stage technique was not ready to do. Independently of any connection with religion and divine service, theatrical illusion had now become all-powerful and developed its own secular magic, the advantages of which even religious drama—in so far as it still lived on in Passion plays and Corpus Christi plays—now exploited.

To be sure, the more extravagantly the ubiquity in time and space of the baroque theatre was presented and enjoyed as a realm of unlimited fantasy and illusion in Court and popular performances, the more natural and normal it came to appear. For, after all, it was only a freedom and mobility of illusion, of the stage scene, of outward, material form, and it happened that the plot and those presenting it no longer paid much heed to it. "One does not know," says Sarasin, in his *Discours de la Tragédie* (1639), "whether the actors are speaking in the houses or on the streets; the stage is like a public hall that is meant for nobody in particular, and where anyone can roam around at will."[12]

The multiplicity and, above all, the quick succession of scenes led to vagueness and confusion; the large number of time-bound contemporary scenes brought chronological bewilderment. The excessive colorfulness and variety of the illusions went hand in hand with a disorder that bewildered the senses of the spectators, obliging them to cling to the words of the actor in order to learn what was going on. This devaluation of the scenic element finally expressed itself in seating arrangements—the more refined part of the audience took to sitting to the right and left on the stage, thereby partially concealing the decor and narrowing the playing space for the actors.

These and similar abuses would certainly have been eliminated if the French national genius had applied itself steadfastly to the externals of stage decor. But to its credit, it was the first to turn away from it and to aim at bringing out in bold relief the inner mind of man. The learned book drama and reading drama of the humanists and the school plays of the Jesuits had educated the public mind to this. The depreciation of theatrical illusion that was making itself unpleasantly felt, at first only occasionally and incidentally, was turned from a necessity into a virtue by Pierre Corneille.

Corneille deliberately shrouded the periods and scenes of his comedies, tragicomedies, and tragedies more and more in an indeterminate, uniform gray, and adapted them as best he could to the rules of Aristotelian poetry, which the humanists and Academicians had already been discussing and recommending for a whole century.[13] In this he was motivated less by a childish awe of Aristotle and his learned disciples than by his love for the inner spirit of man, by his simplicity, his delight in the power of action and words, and his distrust of outward pomp and the deception of the senses—but ultimately, and indeed above all, because his works imperiously demanded moral sincerity. "Because they were a useful method for the exposition of moral truth, he accepted the unities that were not yet established when he began," writes Gustave Lanson, one of the outstanding Corneille experts.[14]

This *vérité morale* is nothing other than what Benedetto Croce calls the *volontà deliberante* (deliberating will), a quality that emerges as the dominant ideal in Corneille's drama.[15] I would call it the responsibility of the will, the grandeur of which, in fact, no writer has portrayed and sung more gloriously than Corneille. To depict it he uses situations, cases, conflicts, alternatives, and dilemmas such as occur in real life, social, civic, and political. For there is no responsibility of the will in the realm of illusion and fantasy. Away, therefore, with all deception of the senses, all fictitious surprise, all artificial disturbance of the unities of time and place! Only when circumstances are depicted as they really are can the action of such a hero be luminously portrayed in its *hic et nunc*.

Corneille needed a gray wall against which the meaning

and brilliance of his poetry could stand out in bold relief. He had to muster all his strength in order to protect himself and his work from the arts of the producers and stage managers. He did not always succeed in this, and, at times, even he doubted whether his characters would show up sufficiently attractively against such a drab and unappealing background. These little uncertainties, these compromises with the exuberant taste of his time, need not trouble us here. The main point is that he swept from his theater all the enchanting brilliance of a secular and courtly nature, all the transformations and surprises in decor, all the wonders and metamorphoses; he transferred them to the minds and souls of his heroes and to the power of their speech. And he resurrected in their spirits all the glory he had eliminated from their background and environment. In this way the lordly brilliance of the world of the great remained nevertheless on the stage, only no longer as something contrived, an apparatus, so to speak, but as human heroism.

This was the state of things when Racine arrived on the scene, and he had to take it over for good or ill. An austere, color-free stage space, and the inflated characters with their great decisions, self-conscious moral responsibility, and resounding words—this was the heritage left behind by Corneille to the disciple who was destined to overcome his influence.

Racine made little change in the theater; he only fulfilled the testament of the master whom he had so greatly revered,[16] and made it still quieter and more uniform in the matter of place, time, and decor. True, he did away with the Corneillian character, whom he could neither believe in nor make his own, and replaced it by his own version of man. The latter was as far removed from the former as Euripides is from Seneca, as suffering is from action, as feeling and instinct are from reason and will, as natural necessity is from free choice, as sensual involvement is from free and proudly responsible self-determination, as subject is from ruler, and tragic defeat from victory. In view of all this, how could Corneille's stage still be suitable for—or indeed at all adapted to—Racine's version of humanity?

The remarkable thing is that it suited Racine's characters far better than it did Corneille's, for whom, after all, it had been evolved. It has struck all critics possessed of any dramatic sense, from Georges de Scudéry to Lanson and Croce, that the stage seemed somehow too narrow, or too bare, or too unyielding for Corneille's characters, that the people gave the impression of being imprisoned, artificially isolated entities. Corneille, says Croce, is somewhat like an artist who, infatuated with the human body he has drawn, eliminates the background of sky, air, and environment out of which a figure is, after all, meant to grow.[17] Racine, on the other hand—if I may continue with the metaphor—possesses the secret of working the natural and human environment, the whole background, into the fashioning of his characters. Where Corneille draws only hard and sharp outlines, Racine, by soft toning and shading, allows the spiritual bodies to expand, to disappear, to lose themselves in the atmosphere, and to emerge again, wonderfully alive. He works artistically, but without brush or color, without naturalistic detail. The richness and sturdiness of a Lope de Vega or a Shakespeare would seem fearfully clamorous and gaudy on his toneless stage; hence, with the same restraint as Corneille, he has surrendered color and sound almost completely to the actor, and contents himself with giving the light and shade.

Racine's drama definitely does not need to be performed in order to be completely effective. For it awakens in the artistic heart of the actor even more than in the public the urge to self-identification, personification, gesture. For it offers the actor the most beautiful opportunities, the most irresistible attractions, and this precisely because it does not need him, because it has been already thought out and envisaged in terms of the stage. Racine created Andromaque, not really for Du Parc, but out of her—he was filled with and carried away by the sound of her voice, the grace of her figure, by her movements and her glances. His Bérénice has borrowed, received, and taken from Champmeslé more than the actress, with all her arts, could have added to her. And has not his Esther emerged so vividly from the souls of the young girls of Saint-Cyr that she, too, can do without the bodily form that the acting of these girls would give her?

Racine's contemporaries knew a great deal about this. They had the direct vision, whereas we can only judge afterward according to eyewitness testimonies and impressions. We can only say this much: since the stage, as a place or space, had become so poor and austere, the relation of the poet to the stage, which representing the human race, that is, his relations with the theatrical profession as a whole, could become all the more fruitful and exuberant. Without the actors of the Molière troupe and of the Hôtel de Bourgogne, Racine could not have written a single play. From this fact we can see, too, that his writings were far less learned and humanistic than they may appear to the philologically inclined critics. It is just his speeches, the power of his language, his words that replace theatrical effect, and live, not on paper, but in the play. The whole motive force of this theater, its sublimity and solemnity, is supplied by the intellectual and sonic means of the spoken word.

5

Racine's Rhetorical and Poetic Art

When a dramatist allows himself to be led by the actor, his art may easily tend to the impromptu and the masquerade. It is a well-known fact that the *commedia dell'arte* came into being because the professional actors of Italy gained the upper hand over the poets—in fact, supplanted them—just as the professional performers of the mimes and Atellae had done many centuries before.

The plot of the impromtu plays was a rough framework or scenario, planned and agreed upon among the actors. The characters consisted of set types or masks, and it was only in the actual performance that the living words of the moment, with their chance moods, witticisms, gestures, and buffoonery, were poured as it were into these molds. Distribution of roles and teamwork, practice and mood, routine and verve, combined to ensure the success of these virtuoso plays, from which the French dramatists, notably Molière, but even Corneille, too, took their lesson. Molière's work has actually been criticized on the ground that many of his characters are not real persons but masks or clichés, that many of his situations are not spiritually developed but merely copied from pantomimes, and that the actor in him often comes too much to the fore and makes his work impromtu and ephemeral.

And is not the comedy in Racine's *Plaideurs* likewise related to pantomime? Is it not essentially dependent on bodily movement, expressive gestures, and the theatrical temperament of the Italians? Is not the general effect one of *lazzo* and trifling, ennobled into literature though it may be, and raised as high as one will, but no less theatrically conceived for all that? There is no sense in being scandalized at this, because all over France, and indeed all over Europe, the theatrical profession, which had just left the fledgling stage, created a delight in the theater, in theatrical illusion, and in the art of pantomime, which inevitably communicated itself to the dramatic poets and influenced their compositions.

Corneille's *Illusion comique* is one of the most impressive proofs of this. In it we hear:

> Ainsi, tous les acteurs d'une troupe comique,
> Leur poème récité, partagent leur pratique.
> L'un tue, l'autre meurt, l'autre vous fait pitié;
> Mais la scène préside à leur inimitié.
> Leurs vers font leurs combats, leur mort suit leurs paroles;
> Et, sans perdre intérêt en pas un de leurs rôles,
> Le traître et le trahi, le mort et le vivant,
> Se trouvent à la fin amis comme devant. (V, 5)

> Thus, all the actors of a company, their poem recited, share their experience. The one kills, the other dies, the other excites your pity; but the stage presides over their enmity. Their verses are their combats, their death follows their words; and without sacrificing interest in any of their roles, the traitor and the betrayed, the dead and the living, are at the end friends as before.

La scène préside. This convention of the stage, this guild spirit of the professional artist, so palpable in comedy, also extended, more or less, to tragedy. Here too the tendency was to find fixed types and set roles, from which the poet was not permitted to deviate any more than the actors, and a stylized mode of speech.

> Achille déplairoit, moins bouillant et moins prompt:
> J'aime à lui voir verser des pleurs pour un affront. . . .
> Qu'Agamemnon soit fier, superbe, intéressé;
> Que pour ses dieux Enée ait un respect austère;
> Conservez à chacun son propre caractère.
>
> (Boileau, *Art poétique,* III)

> Achilles would displease if he were less hot blooded and hasty: I love to see him shed tears for an affront. . . . Let Agamemnon be proud, haughty, selfish; let Aeneas have an austere respect for his gods; conserve to each his proper character.

Just as Italy produced comedy, Roman and Greek antiquity supplied the types, the molds, and the patterns of tragedy. Achilles, Medea, Phaedra, Nero, and the rest are conditioned and circumscribed in a way not essentially different from Harlequin, Sganarell, Matamore, and Isabelle. The particular *bienséance* required of each is coordinated with his or her gestures, deportment, and mode of expression.

Racine had to reckon with this stereotyped theatrical convention, because even if he himself had succeeded in weaning his public away from it, his actors and actresses would not have gone along with him. Just as the proposed reform of French spelling and orthography in the nineteenth century was defeated by the opposition of the printers, the theatrical profession would probably have refused its help and cooperation to Racine, or at least withheld it tacitly.

But actually Racine had not the least wish to break the traditional tables of the law of stage technique and style, or to demand of any of the contemporary exponents of his art a performance for which they had not been adequately prepared by training and practice. Where the traditions of the actor's art were concerned, he was no innovator. He only continued and maintained, in fact, even restrained, what he found before him in the actor's scope! Hence the external austerity, modesty, and simplicity of his theatrical and linguistic means, which is still deplored and derided by opponents of classicism.

But there is not the least ground for this scorn, because the poverty, or rather the austerity and strict economy, of artistic resources is rendered necessary in the Racinian theater by the amplitude and depth of the spiritual riches. Racine and his characters say little because they have to think and feel so much; they act hesitantly because they are in a ferment of stormy emotions; they behave according to the rules, sedately and conventionally, because they are full of criminality or high-mindedness; they hold fast to tradition because they are victims of the most extraordinary circumstances; they conquer and control themselves because they feel unstable and lost;

their self-discipline is the sheet anchor of their *luxuria,* and their elegant ways the reverse side of their urge toward the other world and eternity. Behind these molds lies an incredibly recondite, all too human humanity.

Speech serves these people in reverse, as it were. It acts as the veil and filter of their souls rather than as its expression and outburst; it expresses the restraint, refinement, and intensification of their feelings rather than their release and outflow. Instead of getting out of their dilemmas by their words, they only talk themselves deeper into them. Instead of convincing their partner in dialogue, they only throw him back on himself. They are better versed in anything at all than in rhetoric and eloquence. How should such deliberate and polished speech react on people of action, on the drama itself, except in an essentially hampering way? It makes the action of the play heavy, grandiose, and oppressive instead of letting it move along easily. If Oreste, Mithridate, or Phèdre did not speak, or spoke differently, if they thrust aside their feelings instead of observing them, illuminating them, lifting them into the spectacle and thus making them monumental, they would be saved. But since they are artistic natures, and brood over their passions with all the wealth and warmth of words, fashion themselves upon them and dwell on them, events move on their stormy way over and past them.

The action, considered on its own without the words, tumbles from reef to reef into the depths; it is not a river, but a waterfall over steps of rock that whip it to foam and only seem to obstruct its course. The lively course of events moves on inexorably toward an early end, which is generally seen from the beginning as inevitable, and is artistically delayed by speeches, misunderstandings, rumors, and the like. Racine's dramas really consist solely of final acts, death struggles, and the execution of long-passed sentences or decrees. For this very reason one must not separate the speech from the action in his case, for without the words the action would only be a flash of lightning, or a fall, or a break, a mere nothing, not a plot. As far as we can see from his prose outline of an "Iphigénie en Tauride"[1] that he had planned, Racine himself conceived action and dialogue as one entity from the beginning. What one might more or less call the versification and the diction, also the attention to scenes in detail, he left for later attention.

First he sketched out a scenario in which he determined, act by act and scene by scene, the situations and events, and at the same time, the content and purpose of all the speeches, dialogues, and conversation that were to take place and the opinions to be expressed in them. "When he had tied up all the scenes one with another, he would say: 'My tragedy is made' counting the rest for nothing," his son reports. But then the "nothing" of the final touch, the linguistic polish of the edifice, would unexpectedly become the chief thing, as is the way with genuine artists, just as in the case of impromptu comedy, the air of improvised production, on which everything depends, seemed a trifling matter while the performance was being prepared. Racine worked like a born and trained professional dramatic producer, in an orderly manner from the whole concept down to the details, from the framework to the decor—not like Victor Hugo, who first set down rhetorical and lyrical highlights in their finished wording, then added the drama as a setting around these poetical gems.

With Racine the speech, the verse, the words are in fact nothing and everything: clear and natural as if they were but grown out of the whole, actualized, and, if you will, improvised from the concerted play of all the forces, that is to say, created by a genuine production of the drama in the imagination of its author. In order to launch a composition in this way, like a seaworthy ship from the slipway, like smithing the iron while it is red, an author must be filled up with linguistic resources, humanistically and philologically educated to the tip of his tongue.

From childhood Racine had had an astounding memory for Latin, Greek, Italian, Spanish, and French verse and phraseology. In his youthful letters we find quotations from Lucretius, Cicero, Virgil, Ovid, Tibulus, Terence, Petronius, Petrarch, Ariosto, Tasso, Cervantes, and others, coming to his mind unbidden and in the right place. These epic, bucolic, and idyllic poets of antiquity were soon joined by the great tragedians. He did not devour these authors thoughtlessly; he savors and enjoys them; they do not become mere learned ballast for him. He abhors philological pedantry as much as ignorance. The practice of quotation is suitable for a preacher, but not for a poet, he wrote to Le Vasseur on March 28, 1662. With the profession of writer in view, he made all his reading, all his study serve the formation of his taste.

It was only the Bible, the Fathers of the Church, and the theologians that he read essentially for the content. Therefore it would be mistaken to believe that his study of the humanities and his philological studies applied only to the forms of language. In exercising his understanding strenuously—on Pindar, for example—he tried to observe very specially the meaning and the ordered sequence of the author's thoughts, and only after that, his style and language. Even in these childish efforts a metaphor or an epithet would strike a deep chord in his spirit. In his notes on Pindar's *Olympic Odes* we read, on the Seventh Ode: "He calls the sun ἅγνον θεόν because it purifies everything with its rays,"[2] a thought that recurs twenty-five years later in the tragedy of the granddaughter of the sun. What moves him especially deeply again and again in the *Odyssey* is the relation between human beings and the gods. The first verses that he finds worth writing down are the words of a god:

> Ὢ πόποι, οἷον δή νυ θεοὺς βροτοί αἰτιόωνται!

> (Alas, how falsely the mortals often accuse us heavenly ones!
> They say every misfortune comes from us, and yet they have sufferings
> Brought on themselves by their folly, over and above fate.)[3]

The mental attitude of Homer's characters, and the customs in which it expresses itself, impress him just as deeply as the beauty and grace of the composition. For instance: "It is a beautiful thing to see how hospitality is practiced in the *Odyssey*, and the veneration with which all strangers are received." Thereupon he proceeds to collect examples and expressions of this beautiful attitude, for example:

> πρός γαρ Διός εἰσιν ἅπαντες
> ετοί τε πτωχοί τέ.

> Every beggar and guest
> Is a messenger of Zeus.[4]

Or: "The first thing one did was to drink in honor of the gods, such as Jupiter the hospitable one, and some other gods; and even of some of one's best friends if these were dead or absent, as one sees everywhere in Homer and in other authors."[5] On the verse

> *ἀλλ' ἤτοι μὲν ταῦτα θεῶν ἐν γούνασι κεῖται*

> But that surely rests in the lap of the gods

he remarks: "This verse is sufficiently frequent in Homer to betoken the providence of the gods." The prayer of the shipwrecked Odysseus impresses him particularly:

> Hear me, O ruler, whoever you may be! One who calls upon you approaches,
> Who flees from the deep waters, before the threats of Poseidon.
> Even sacred before the eternal gods is the wanderer,
> Who on his forlorn way, a supplicant, comes, as now
> I touch your stream and knees with sighing mouth.[6]

"This is what Seneca translated by the words: *Res est sacra miser* in the verses that he made during his exile. And this sentiment is all the more beautiful for being impressed upon the heart by nature itself. Thus, Ulysses says: 'I come to your waters and to your knees.' To your waters, *σόν τε ῥοόν*, as to a river, *σά τε γούνατ'*, as to a god. . . . They revered the supplicants and did not allow anyone to touch them. That is to be seen everywhere in the story —in the refuges, in the temples, in the palaces, beside the statues of the princes."[7]

In short, young Racine's study of Homer is essentially a consideration of the composition as an expression of a way of thinking. And when he comes on forms of feeling and faith that remind him of Holy Scripture, his heart rejoices. For instance, the Phaeacian king's idea that Odysseus might be a god who is putting the hospitality of men to the test (*Odyssey*, VII, 199 ff.): "One would think that Homer took this beautiful sentiment from the books of Moses—that the gods sometimes assume the form of travelers in order to test the hospitality of those who serve them, and who are favored by them, as one sees in the story of Abraham."[8]

However, these and similar points of agreement definitely do not lead him into medieval moralizings and spiritualizings of

Homer's world of fable. He emphatically rejects this kind of exegesis in his reflections on the song of Circe.[9] His method of consideration concerns itself explicitly with the artistic aspect, and the expression in words of human, but particularly of ethical and religious, feelings and sentiments. He grasps with a fresh eye the cohesion, the closely interwoven unity, of ethos and style. If only Homer and the tragic dramatists were read in all schools with the eyes of a young Racine!

Because he regards content and form, mental attitude and speech, as essentially one whole, he grasps particularly eagerly the expressive gestures, the accents denoting feeling, the verbal tones of the heart of the Homeric characters. He cannot admire sufficiently the loving nature of the conversation between Odysseus and Nausicaa. "Actually, that address is one of the most beautiful passages in Homer, and one of the most gallant. It is completely in keeping with a sensitive and adroit mind like Ulysses', desiring to gain some credit with that beautiful unknown woman."[10]

Of Homer he says: "One would think that he changes his style in each place, so much does he keep the character of the people."[11]

It was inevitable that only those scenes, verses, and expressions that were full of character, significant of a mental attitude, pregnant with feeling, and spiritually meaningful would remain permanently in Racine's memory. This shows the impulsive, simple, human, and deeply emotional heart with which he communed with other minds through books. His attitude toward the classical authors was childlike rather than literary, and he was almost as familiar with them as if they had written in his native tongue. That is why his dramatic poetry, even when it sounds almost like a word-for-word rendering of Euripides, Virgil, or Seneca, never gives the impression of being learned or of being non-French. The texts of his dramas have been lavishly glossed by industrious publishers and commentators with Latin, Greek, and French material for purposes of comparison. By now we know most of the sources, also the borrowed or unoriginal terms used by the highly educated poet, and we see that he hardly ever copies down or "translates" in the philological sense of the word. There is no learned antiquarianism, there are no technical expressions in his work—apart from those used for the purpose of comical effect in *Les Plaideurs*. But in his youthful works he had in many cases adopted the gallant and precious manner of speech then fashionable. Apart from these, the dominant speech of his works is the current conversational language of courtly society, cultured circles, and good families, a purified language of the heart, the reason, and good mores.[12]

To fall in with the prevailing custom and remain unobtrusive—such is the negative and positively prosaic ideal of this style. Racine's poetical language has no striking characteristics. It is a secularized style, modeled on the conversation customary in the polite world, and it achieves its sublimity and solemnity by renouncing the carnal, the coarse, and the strange. Just as the renunciation of sensual pleasure is the guiding star of his poetry, it is likewise that of his language, with its incomparable worldly, supraworldly chastity and purity, its inwardness and restraint, that seem dreary and tedious to those of uncultivated taste, and noble to the cultured.

While still a youth, Racine knew what he was giving up in renouncing naturalism and strong language in speech, and why he was giving it up. At twenty-two he wrote as gloss to the *Odyssey,* V, 234 ff.: "How exact Homer is in describing the least particulars, to which Greek is well adapted, whereas Latin is much more reserved, and does not amuse itself with such little things. The language is undoubtedly more sterile, and has not words that express things as felicitously as Greek; for one would say that there is nothing low in Greek, and that the most vile things are expressed nobly in it. It is the same with our language as with Latin, for it goes to extremes to avoid descending to details, because ears are sensitive and cannot tolerate low things such as an axe, a saw, or a brace being mentioned in a serious discourse. Italian, on the other hand, resembles Greek in that it expresses everything, as one can see in Ariosto, who in his way is a character comparable with Homer."

And his gloss on the *Odyssey,* VII, 216 ff., runs: "Our language would not tolerate, in an epic poem, this manner of speaking, which seems proper only to burlesque."[13] And on the *Odyssey,* X, 410 ff.: "These words about calves and cows are not at all shocking in the Greek as they are in our language, which can tolerate hardly anything and which would not tolerate that eclogues should be made about cows, as Theocritus did, nor that one should speak of Ulysses' swineherd as if he were an heroic personage. But these niceties are real weaknesses."[14]

According to this, Racine felt very clearly that the French avoidance of the everyday in the literary language then current was a literary weakness, a preciousness; nevertheless he fell in with it. At first, no doubt, out of motives dictated by the world, by society, by fashion, by national feelings, he complied with the *délicatesses* and *foiblesses* of his period. More or less in the spirit of his Parthénice, he fell in with the courtly attitude and tastes:

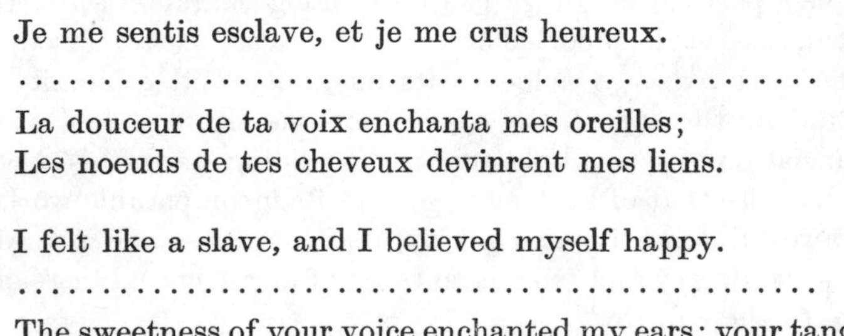

Je me sentis esclave, et je me crus heureux.

. . . .

La douceur de ta voix enchanta mes oreilles;
Les noeuds de tes cheveux devinrent mes liens.

I felt like a slave, and I believed myself happy.

. . . .

The sweetness of your voice enchanted my ears; your tangles of hair became my bonds.

But the more the tragic thought of renunciation of the world in the midst of the world took possession of him, the more his style lost its lushness and affectation. His demure and elegant restraint of speech progressively gave way to a consciously masculine and exalted intellectuality. Without noticeable alteration of either the construction or the vocabulary, the courtly style of speech acquired an increasingly serious and deep tone from the tragic attitude of mind that began to dominate and permeate it more and more. The purification of his language proceeds step by step unobtrusively from *La Thébaïde* to *Athalie,* for it is accomplished more in the spiritual content than in the fabric of the words.

Racine troubled little about grammatical rules and linguistic purism. "Faultless writing," says a perceptive Frenchman of today, "consists, for us, in making words into sentences according to a certain usage which is laid down in easily obtainable textbooks, and keeps us on the right track by means of elaborate prohibitions. This monotonous kind of faultlessness definitely was not characteristic of our classical authors. They were content to be guided more by the spirit than by the letter of a syntax that was still flexible and capable of taking the imprint of the individual on its comparative indeterminateness. Vauglas advised rather than ordered that Père Bouhours should publish his rules of the language only later; and the rules of the participles, for example, did not become valid before 1704. Grammar was formerly a philosophy, not a code with endless qualifications and exceptions."[15] The rules of syntax may not have been exactly a philosophy for Racine, but they were something of the kind; a matter, not merely of good taste, but, still more, of good, simple, and elevated mind.

Racine's attitude in the matter of aesthetics is a touchy and delicate one, but we must make an attempt to understand it in the light of the history of style, and take it at its face value.

Just as the theater of classical tragedy had to work its way laboriously upward to simplicity from the pomp and the scene shiftings of the Baroque theatre, the language of classical tragedy had likewise to work its way out of the atmosphere of preciosity. An exaggerated, odd, and striking tension between the sensual and the intellectual quality of the language was a characteristic of the precious mode of expression. Writers loved to link together meanings which of their nature were contradictory, for instance: *sagesse ignorante, innocemment coupable, sombrement éclairci.* They loved, above all, to link the coarse with the fine, the visible with the abstract, the natural with the intellectual. The ears became *les portes de l'entendement* (the doors of understanding), water became *le miroir céleste* (the celestial mirror), the eyes became *les hotelleries de la beauté* (the hostelries of beauty), and so on. They spoke of *cheveux d'un blond hardi* (hair of a bold blond), *secheresse de conversation* (dryness of conversation), the *anatomie d'un coeur* (the anatomy of a heart), a *réputation malade* (a sick reputation), *une âme paralytique* (paralytic soul).[16] The effect lay in the surprise coupling of heterogeneous worlds of meaning. The expression was expanded, stretched, and inflated to the utmost—and this not only where the matter was important and exalted—with outbreaks of merriment and wit and the noisy play of the intellect. As long as both worlds of meaning counterbalance each other, the impression remains doubtful, the style impure, and one does not know whether a joker or a hero is speaking. For instance, there is that passage in Cyrano de Bérgérac's *Agrippine,* in which the widow of Germanicus glorifies her husband's victory:

Déjà notre Aigle en l'air balançoit le tonnerre
Dont il devoit brûler la moitié de la terre,

Quand on vint rapporter au grand Germanicus
Qu'on voyait l'Allemand, sous de vastes écus,
Marcher par un chemin couvert de nuits sans nombre:
"L'éclat de notre acier en dissipera l'ombre!"
Dit-il. Et pour la charge il lève le signal.
Sa voix donne la vie à des corps de métal.
Le Romain par torrents se répand dans la plaine;
Le Colosse du Nord se soutient à grand peine:
Son énorme grandeur ne lui sert seulement
Qu'à montrer à la Parque un plus grand logement;
Et, tandis qu'on heurtoit ces murailles humaines;
Pour épargner le sang des Légions romaines,
Mon Héros, ennuyé du combat qui traînoit,
Se cachoit presque entier dans les coups qu'il donnoit.
Là, des bras emportés; là, des têtes brisées. . .
(*Mort d'Agrippine* I, 1)

Our Eagle was already balancing in the air the thunderbolt with which he was to burn half the earth, when someone came to tell great Germanicus that the Germans, under enormous shields, could be seen marching along a road covered in endless night; "The flash of our steel will scatter the shadows!" he said. And he raised the signal for the charge. His voice animated bodies and metal. The Romans spread in torrents over the plains; the Colossus of the North maintained himself with difficulty; his enormous size merely served to show the Parca a roomier lodging, and during the clash against these human walls, weary of the combat's length, my Hero, to spare the blood of the Roman legions, hid himself almost completely in the blows he gave. There, severed arms; there, broken heads. . . .

Now, with Corneille the intellectual values of the words gain the upper hand, and the sensual values fade.[17]

Les palmes dont je vois ta tête si couverte
Semblent porter écrit le destin de ma perte. (*Cid*, II, 2)

The palms I see your head so covered with, seem to carry the message of my fated defeat.

The physical has disappeared from the *palmes* and the *tête:* one does not see leaves with an inscription, nor a head bedecked with palms; one feels and thinks of *palmes* as a value, as fame and glory, and of *tête* as head and dignity. One does not meet any witty combinations of incompatible mental pictures, but a bleak succession of exalted thoughts associated with values.

> Cet effort sur ma flamme à mon honneur est dû.

> My honor demands that I make this effort over my ardor.

The metaphor of the flame combined with ethical values such as *honneur* and *effort* cannot develop its sensual content, and only points to flaming passion; it therefore becomes, on its part, something spiritual and ethical. In Corneille we find a group of favorite words, such as *bras, main, fer, flamme, palme, laurier, glace,* that become stripped of their visible connotation owing to the context in which they occur, and are forced upward, as it were, into the region of noble sentiments, ideas, and ideals. The disembodying apotheosis was not always successful. One observes regrettable lapses into a dubious earthiness, more especially in the works of his earlier years and his old age. For instance:

> Je l'ai vu tout sanglant, au milieu des batailles,
> Se faire un beau rempart de mille funérailles.

> In the midst of battles, I saw him, all bloody, make a bulwark of a thousand bodies . . .

which he rightly altered later to read:

> Je l'ai vu tout couvert de sang et de poussière
> Porter partout la mort dans une ermée entière.

> I saw him, all covered with blood and dust, carry death everywhere into an entire army.

Instead of sating our imagination with external manifestations, and letting us rest in contemplation of them, Corneille stirs it up and excites in it the thirst for the suprasensual and eternal things.

His style is a stimulant to the feelings rather than full of feeling itself.

To this strenuous flight among the heights Racine's language brought a restful, lilting, gently gliding motion, and a pendular descent toward the earth. It was not that his style plunged back into a wealth of metaphors and colors. He held to the heights that had been reached, took over the idealized stage language of the master, and made no decisive effort to re-establish in their original literal, material meaning Corneille's *feux, flammes, fers, mains, bras, noeuds, larmes*. Such miracles of rejuvenation he left to the whimsical and archaic fable-making of his nontragic friend La Fontaine. He preserved the conventions of the tragic style. In the dramas of his later period one can even find verses where the curve of meaning still runs similarly to that of Corneille. For instance:

> Et sur mes foibles mains fondant leur délivrance,
> Il me fit d'un Empire accepter l'espérance . . .
> (*Esther* I, 1)

> And basing their deliverance on my frail hands, he made me accept the hope of an empire . . .

where one sees no hands, but thinks of defenselessness; or

> Le jour approche où le Dieu des armées
> Va de son bras puissant faire éclater l'appui. (Ibid.)

> The day is coming on which the God of armies will with his powerful arm make his support shine forth.

Just as there are remnants of preciousness in Corneille, there are remnants of Corneille in Racine; but they do not constitute the dominant trait of his style. His basic nature consists not in the transcendence of his material, but in the reincarnation of the intellectual and ethical meanings of the words. While Corneille presses out and exposes to view the idea behind the sensual word, the idea itself bends down, as it were, to Racine's wording, penetrating and warming it, lighting it up, and elevating it.

> Dieu tient le coeur des rois entre ses mains puissantes.

> God holds the hearts of kings between his powerful hands.

This is an expression that can be just as well thought of as seen; it is seen in the measure that it is devoutly felt. It originates from the Biblical text *Cor regis in manu Domini* (The king's heart in the hand of the Lord; Proverbs, XXI, 1), but Racine has made it still more vivid by his *tient, entre,* and *puissantes.*

> De mes larmes au ciel j'offrais le sacrifice—
>
> I offered the sacrifice of my tears to heaven—

One sees the figure of a suppliant woman without the material details of a sacrificial action holding one's gaze, for the natural value of the words veils and transfigures the image they convey. What we contemplate through the color of a feeling shows us only a few isolated sensual features. But these suffice to enable us to guess at a whole picture, which they suggest. I quote again from the first scene of *Esther,* for almost every verse is designed to strengthen our mental picture.

> Esther, disois-je, Esther dans la poupre est assise,
> La moitié de la terre à son sceptre est soumise,
> Et de Jérusalem l'herbe cache les murs!
> Sion, repaire affreux de reptiles impurs,
> Voit de son temple saint les pierres dispersées,
> Et du Dieu d'Israel les fêtes sont cessées.
>
> "Esther," I said, "Esther is clothed in purple, and half of the earth is under her scepter. And grass hides the walls of Jerusalem! Zion, the terrible haunt of impure reptiles, sees the stones of its holy temple scattered, and the festivals of the God of Israel are no more."

Is not everything here observed from the contrast between the ideas of brilliance and wretchedness? Esther robed in purple, of which the rich magnificence flames up for a moment; the scepter, the grass, the ruins emerge before the inner eye, only to be silted over, as it were, by the terrible thought of a people forsaken by God.

> Cependant mon amour pour notre nation
> A rempli ce palais de filles de Sion,

Jeunes et tendres fleurs, par le sort agitées,
Sous un ciel étranger comme moi transportées.

Nevertheless my love for our nation has filled this palace with daughters of Zion, young and tender flowers, shaken by fate and like myself brought under this foreign sky.

A sense of value and a mental picture are combined in *fleurs*, and *sort* is fate and a wind at the same time. Even purely abstract things such as *pudeur* assume a sensual color in Racine's work.

Quelle aimable pudeur sur leur visage est peinte!
(*Esther*, I, 2)

What charming modesty is painted on her face!

Beauté becomes concrete:

Ciel! quel nombreux essaim d'innocentes beautés
S'offre à mes yeux en foule et sort de tous côtés!

Heaven! what numberless swarms of innocent beauties crowd before my eyes and come from all all sides!

By means of association of ideas, by sequence, rhythm, and sound, Racine can make the poorest and palest words come alive.

With him syntax, rhythm, and rhyme all work together to pour fluency and harmony into the commonplace and positively prim conversational speech of his characters. It is a matter of literary history that Racine also took these means over from Corneille, and to some extent from Rotrou, as well. He did not alter anything in the scheme of the alexandrine, nor in the alternation of masculine and feminine pairs of rhymes. He only made the caesuras, the stresses, the rhymes a little lighter and softer, and he arranged the order of words somewhat less obstrusively.

It might perhaps be interesting to trace one by one these modest stylistic reductions, and to document them by comparisons. The fundamental difference between the two, and the change in style from Corneille to Racine, would thus be checked and verified bit by bit, a meticulous task that would produce more or less the same result every time, namely, the perception that Racine proceeded less mechanically and essentially more sensitively in his use of the existing possibilities of the dramatic verse of his time, and of his domain of art. How should it be otherwise?

With Corneille, the poet of the responsible will, the supremely important thing is that the hero should rise above the stage of reflection and deliberation to definitive decision; that the blindness of emotions should be rejected, clear judgment reached, and the path to action freed. Hence the pauses, the stresses, the rhymes take on a meditative emphasis, and the speech feels its way forward as if by fits and starts. Unruly passions are held back, stemmed, tried, and sampled, until thought takes its place at their head. The whole inner life appears inverted, its spontaneity checked, and the conscious and deliberate spirit quickened.

In Racine the process is more or less the opposite in its course. Reflection comes too late, and feeling plunges forward blindly. Speech comes in a stream; the pauses, the stresses, the high notes, the rhymes, all seem to become breathing waves of the heart's blood, and lend the verse a sensuously rather than a reflectively divided rhythm. In place of the stressed effect that characterizes Corneille, Racine's rhyme takes on the value of a natural resonance and ring; the order of words follows the impetus of the feelings instead of the onward march of decisions.

I have sought to trace these historically documented differences in style to philosophical positions. Corneille, it is said, portrays the Cartesian and Racine the Pascalian or Jansenistic man on the stage. The fact is, however, that both dramatists were very little preoccupied with philosophy; neither of them ever tied himself down to any given philosophical system. The Cartesian man is essentially a contemplative person; Corneille's characters are men of action. The Pascalian or Arnauldian man is immersed in theology and mysticism; Racine's characters live and suffer in the world. True literature seldom emerges from the study cells of thinkers and scholars. Spiritual connections that can be proved by psychology and social history are of course to be found among contemporaries and compatriots. And we ourselves have spun ingenious yarns of this kind between the hermits' cells of Port-Royal and the boards of the Racinian theater. But Racine's work as such really has nothing to do with all this.

Racine's tragedies deserve to be studied more closely in every way—critically, and also in the light of social and cultural history—in order to clear the way for fuller understanding. If all this effort brings us face to face with his work at last, then it only remains for us to hear it, to listen to it as the voice of a real person, a man who could well declare to us, in the words of Goethe's Iphigenia:

> Nicht Worte sind es, die nur blenden sollen;
> Ich habe dir mein tiefstes Herz entdeckt.

> These are no words meant only to dazzle;
> I have laid bare to you my inmost heart.

Chronological Table

Racine's Life

1639 December 22: Racine baptized with the name of Jean in La Ferté-Milon (Champagne).

1641 January 28: Death of Racine's mother, Jeanne, nee Sconin.

1642 November 4: Second marriage of Jean Racine's father, to Madeleine Vol.

1643 February 6: Death of Racine's father. The paternal grandparents, Jean Racine and his wife, Marie, nee des Moulins, take charge of the infant orphan.

1649 September: Death of the grandfather, Jean Racine. The grandmother retires to Port-Royal des Champs, where her daughter Agnès is a religious, and places her grandson in the Collège at Beauvais as a boarder.

1655 Autumn: Racine is received into the Ecole des Granges, Port-Royal, conducted by Nicole and Lancelot.

1658 October: Racine tranfers from the Ecole des Granges to the Collège d'Harcourt, where his father's cousin, Nicolas Vitard, superintendent of the household of the Duc de Luynes, takes charge of him, and eventually, about 1660, takes him to live with in the Hôtel de Luynes. There he becomes friendly with the Abbé Le Vasseur, and also meets La Fontaine.

1661 (November) until 1663: Racine lives with his uncle Antoine Sconin, Vicar-General of the Bishop of Uzès, who tries to secure a benefice for his nephew and to persuade him to take Holy Orders.

1663 Racine returns to Paris, at first living in the Hôtel de Luynes.

1663 August 12: Death of his grandmother, Marie des Moulins.

1663 Writes literary compositions for the Court. Meets Chapelain. His friendship with Boileau begins. First attends Court. Commences writing dramas.

1666 He breaks with Port-Royal.

1666–1677 Writes his masterpieces of secular drama.

1673 January 12: Racine is elected a member of the Académie Française.

1677 Racine becomes reconciled with Port-Royal. Renounces the theater. Marries Catherine des Romanet on June, 1677. Is appointed *Historiographe du Roy.* In this capacity he accompanies the French army in spring 1678 to Ghent, in 1683 to Alsace, in 1687 to Luxembourg, in 1691, 1692, and 1693 to Mons, Namur, and the Netherlands.

1689–1691 Commissioned by Madame de Maintenon, he composes the religious dramas *Esther* and *Athalie* for performance by the pupils of the Academy for Young Ladies at Saint-Cyr.

1690 He is appointed a *Gentilhomme du Roy.*

1698 Incurs the displeasure of Louis XIV.

1699 April 21: Death of Racine.

Racine's Works

1655–1658 Odes in Praise of Port-Royal

1659 (?) *Les Bains de Vénus,* a composition in the galant style, now lost

1660 An Ode, *La Nymphe de la Seine*

1660–1663 Humanistic and theological studies and translations from the Greek

1660–1661 Lost works on the Tragédies of *Amasie, Les Amours d'Ovide,* and *Théagene et Chariclée*

1661 or 1662 (?) *Stances à Parthénice*

1662–1663 *La Thébaïde,* tragedy

1663 Ode, *Sur la convalescence du Roi*
Ode, *La Renommée aux Muses*
1664 *Chapelain décoiffé*, a parody, in collaboration with Boileau, La Fontaine, and Molière
1665 *Alexandre*, a tragedy
1666 *Lettre à l'Auteur des Imaginaires* and *Lettre aux deux apologistes de l'auteur des Imaginaires*, polemic against Port-Royal
1667 *Andromaque*
1668 *Les Plaideurs*
1669 *Britannicus*
1670 *Bérénice*
1672 *Bajazet*
1673 *Mithridate*
1674 *Iphigénie*; plan for an *Iphigénie en Tauride* (?)
1675 (?) Fragments from Aristotle's *Poetry* translated from Greek
1677 *Phèdre*
1678 Discourse at the Académie Française on the occasion of the reception of the Abbé Colbert
From 1678: Engaged in studies and preliminary drafts for the History of Louis XIV, commissioned by the king from his royal historiographer
1680 Worked in Collaboration with Boileau on the libretto of an opera, *Phaéton*
From 1683 Studies and Works for the Académie Royale des Inscriptions et Médailles
1680(?) Translates Plato's *Symposium* from the Greek
1685 Gives an address at the Académie Française on the occasion of the reception of Thomas Corneille and of Bergeret
1685 *Idylle sur la Paix*, set to music by Lully
1689 *Esther*
1691 *Athalie*
1694 *Cantiques spirituels*
1693–1698 (?) *Abregé de l'Histoire de Port-Royal*

Notes

CHAPTER 1

1. *Oeuvres de J. Racine,* ed. Paul Mesnard ("Les grands écrivains de la France"), 2d ed. (Paris, 1923, VII, 168). I always quote from this edition.
2. *Oeuvres,* VII, 85 ff., 135, 141 ff., 151, 154, 260, and I, 302.
3. *Oeuvres,* VI, 427 ff.
4. *Oeuvres,* I, 214 ff.
5. It is known that Malherbe sought good and genuine linguistic usage not only among the "courtiers," but just as much among the "porters of the Port Saint-Jean."
6. The Duc de Lynes, in whose palace Racine lived at that time together with his "uncle" Nicolas Vitard.
7. *Oeuvres,* VI, 392.
8. *Oeuvres,* VI, 476.
9. "Nothing of the poet in his business intercourse, and everything of the gentleman, the modest man, and—toward the end—the man of means," the Duc de Saint-Simon writes of him in his *Memoirs*. And the old nobleman was an authority on courtly manners and customs such as only a master of ceremonies can be.
10. *Oeuvres,* VI, 497 f.
11. On August 13, 1687, he wrote to him: "The more I see the number of my friends decreasing, the more conscious do I become of the few who remain to me. And to be quite frank, it seems to me that there is hardly anyone left to me

but you"; *Oeuvres,* VI, 600. Boileau replies no less cordially: "I feel capable of leaving everything except you"; *ibid.,* p. 605; and "I shall tell you something more; it is this—that without your consideration I do not believe that I would ever have seen Paris again, where I can conceive of no other pleasure than that of seeing you again"; *ibid.,* p. 619. See also Boileau's famous "Epître VII à Monsieur Racine."

12. *Oeuvres,* I, 351.
13. *Oeuvres,* VII, 279.
14. *Oeuvres,* V, 622 ff.
15. Letter to the author of *Hérésies Imaginaires* and the *Deux Visionnaires,* and letter to two apologists of Port-Royal, in *Oeuvres,* IV, 259 ff.
16. This second reply was published only long after Racine's death, in Volume IV of the works of Nicolas Despréaux, at The Hague, 1722.
17. So Jean Baptiste, Racine's eldest son, tells us; see *Oeuvres,* IV, 266 ff.
18. *Oeuvres,* IV, 286 ff.
19. "After all, this famous conversion was no more than the natural end of a stormy youth," says one of the best recent Racine experts, Gonzague Truc, in *Le cas Racine* (Paris, 1922), p. 50.
20. Letter to Boileau, May 30, 1693, in *Oeuvres,* VII, 78.
21. *Oeuvres,* VI, 480 ff.
22. *Oeuvres,* VI, 485.
23. *Oeuvres,* I, 211.
24. *Oeuvres,* VI, 559.
25. *Oeuvres,* IV, 364.
26. *Oeuvres,* IV, 375.
27. *Oeuvres,* V, 178 ff. *Ad Solis instar, beaturus suo calore ac lumine Galliam Galliaeque amicos.*
28. *Oeuvres,* V, 123 ff.
29. *Oeuvres,* V, 125.
30. The are numerous proofs and examples of this in the *Précis historique des campagnes de Louis XIV,* which he apparently composed together with Boileau; see *Oeuvres,* V, 243 ff. Also *Relation du Siège de Namur, ibid.,* pp. 312 ff.
31. See *Oeuvres,* V, 3 ff. and 17 ff., from which one can get an insight into Racine's part in producing the medals commemorating the principal events of the reign of Louis the Great, with historical explanations (Paris, 1702).

32. The country house and gardens of Marly-le-Roi were destroyed in the Revolution.
33. *Oeuvres,* VI, 609 ff.
34. *Oeuvres,* I, 299.
35. *Oeuvres,* VII, 230 ff.
36. *Oeuvres,* VII, 227 ff.
37. *Oeuvres,* I. 276. Louis Racine even predated his father's translation of Plato, placing it before the conversion, to avoid having to admit a relapse into worldly pursuits; see *Oeuvres,* V, 428 ff.
38. Cf. *Oeuvres,* I, 109 ff. Boileau tells of this relapse with his accustomed candor: "Madame de Montespan and her sister, Madame de Thiange, tired of M. Quinault's operas, suggested to the King that they should get one composed by Racine, who promised quite readily to do what they wanted, momentarily forgetting what he had agreed with me several times already, that to make a good opera is impossible because music is unable to express a narrative. . . . I pointed this out to him when he told me of his assignment, and he admitted that I was right, but said he had gone too far to turn back. He actually began an opera there and then, the subject being the fall of Phaeton. He even wrote some initial verses of it, and he recited them to the King, who seemed pleased with them. But as M. Racine only undertook this work reluctantly, he insisted that he would never finish it unless I worked with him. And he declared, to begin with, that I would have to compose the prologue. In vain I pointed out to him how little talent I had for works of this kind and that I had never written love poems; he stuck to his point and said that he would see I was ordered to do it by the King. I began, accordingly, considering what I could do. . . . That's the subject of my prologue, on which I worked for three or four days with considerable distaste, while M. Racine, with no less aversion, continued to work out the plan of his opera, assisted by constant advice from me. We were engaged on this wretched work, which I hardly think we could have got out of very well, when suddenly a happy incident delivered us from it. The incident was that, M. Quinault having presented himself to the King with tears in his eyes and pointed out how affronted he would feel if he were not permitted to work any more to entertain His Majesty, the King, touched with compassion,

declared roundly to the ladies I have mentioned, that he could not bring himself to cause Quinault this offense. *Sic nos servavit Apollo.*" Boileau, *Fragment d'un prologue d'opèra.*

39. *Oeuvres,* IV, 79 ff.
40. *Oeuvres,* I, 150.
41. *Oeuvres,* VII, 277 ff.
42. *Oeuvres,* I, 210.
43. *Oeuvres,* VII, 21, 71 ff., 285, 295.
44. This remark refers to Racine's eldest daughter, Marie Catherine, who, however, married later, at her father's wish.
45. *Oeuvres,* VII, 330; I, 320, 125 ff.
46. *Oeuvres,* I, 276.
47. See his letters on these matters, *Oeuvres,* VII, 290 ff. and 293 ff.
48. *Oeuvres,* I, 351 n.

Chapter 2

1. *Introduction à la vie dévote,* ch. III and XXIII.
2. The connections between Saint Francis de Sales and the Jesuit order, and the fundamental thoughts concerning asceticism in the world and beauty of soul common to both, were brought out particularly well by Olaf Homèn, *Studier i fransk Klassicism* (Helsinki, 1914), pp. 91 ff.
3. Henri Bremond has described it thoroughly and praised it lavishly under the name of *Humanisme dévot* in his *Histoire littéraire du sentiment religieux en France,* Vol. I (Paris, 1923).
4. I say favored, not produced.
5. Fritz Adler, *Racine als Mensch und Künstler* (diss. Leipzig; publ. Dresden, 1915), seems to me not to have recognised this relationship correctly. For he makes out that the poet, whose works he had been interpreting all his life as a literary historian, was perpetually vacillating between God and the world.
6. See Josefa Juise Prückner, "Port-Royal und die spanische Mystik" (diss. Munich, 1921).
7. Besides the perceptive cultural and spiritual history contained in Sainte-Beuve's *Port-Royal,* it may suffice to refer to the apologetic work of Augustin Gazier, *Histoire générale du mouvement janséniste* (Paris, 1924), and to the essentially polemi-

cal one of H. Bremond, *L'école de Port-Royal*, Vol. IV of his *Histoire littéraire du sentiment religieux en France* (Paris, 1923).

8. *Athalie*, I, 4. Note how the thoughts on the order of nature and of the moral law, separated into vv. 6 and 8 in Psalm 18, are fused into one by Racine.
9. *Esther*, II, 8.
10. *Oeuvres*, IV, 178 and 228. A whole series of couplets of similar style and content, ascribed partly to Racine and partly to his friends, for instance:

    Et contre la justice et contre la raison
    Je vais condamner un grand homme;
    Mais d'un crime qui plaît à Rome
    On a facilement pardon.

    or:

    Ayant signé le Formulaire,
    Un ami qui ne peut se taire
    M'accuse d'infidélité:
    "Pourquoi, dit-il, pourquoi par une lâche feinte
    Abandonner la vérité,
    Puisqu'elle est éternelle et sainte?
    —Vous voulez donc, lui dis-je, en savoir le pourquoi?
    C'est parce qu'étant sainte et qu'étant éternelle,
    Je ne dois rien craindre pour elle,
    Et je ne dois penser qu'à moi."

11. *Oeuvres*, IV, 156 ff.
12. *Oeuvres*, VII, 370. It continues: "I very humbly beg the Mother Abbess and the nuns to please grant me this honour, of which I recognize myself to be most unworthy owing to the scandals of my past life and the poor use I have made of the excellent education once received in this house and the great examples of piety and penitence I have seen there, and of which I have been a fruitless admirer. But the more I have offended God, the greater is my need of the prayers of a community so holy, to draw His mercy upon me. I also ask the Reverend Mother Abbess and the nuns kindly to accept the sum of eight hundred pounds that I have ordered to be given to them after my death.

    "Made in my study in Paris, the 10th October, 1698."
13. Sainte-Beuve, *Port-Royal*, VI, 157.

CHAPTER 3

1. That it is just the same in England can be gathered from Lytton Strachey's brilliant Racine apologia in *Books and Characters, French and English* (London, 1924), pp. 3 ff. It is otherwise in Italy, where Racine is understood and valued as a poet of humanism; see Mario Fubini's clever book, *J. Racine e la critica delle sue tragedie* (Turin, 1925).
2. *H. von Kleist* (Berlin, 1922), pp. 73 ff.
3. The influence of *Pompée* on *Alexandre* is unmistakable. In both plays the heroic and gallant protagonist appears on the stage only in the third act, after admiration for him has been sufficiently prepared. With triumphant grandeur he humiliates the vanquished and pays homage to those he loves. See also F. Gundolf, *Cäsar* (Berlin, 1924), pp. 193 ff.
4. It is certainly difficult for the French public to believe in an "uncoquettish" Andromaque. "Andromaque est-elle coquette?" (Is Andromache coquettish?) was circularized as an inquiry by great French daily papers years ago. See Jules Lemaître, *Jean Racine*, 9th ed. (Paris, 1908), pp. 142 ff.
5. See his preface, "Au lecteur." Regarding the relation of *Les Plaideurs* to their sources, see Pierre Kohler, *Autour de Molière. L'esprit classique et la Comédie* (Paris, 1925), pp. 189 ff.
6. *Op. cit.* p. 169.
7. Second Preface to *Britannicus*.
8. Cf. F. Brunière, *Histoire de la littérature française classique*, II, 563 ff.
9. If one examines, for instance, the last scene of Act IV with some sense of humor, one discovers all kinds of hidden charms in it.
10. The story that Princess Henrietta of England invited the two poets to compete on this subject, is probably fictitious; see G. Michaut, *La Bérénice de Racine* (1907), pp. 59 ff. Auguste Dorchain, in his *Pierre Corneille* (Paris, 1918), p. 438, holds firmly to this story. Moreover, he takes *Tite et Bérénice* as a tragicomedy.
11. Similarly Mario Fubini, "Umanismo, Teatro, Poesia nell'opera di Jean Racine," in *La Cultura*, IV (Rome, 1924), 70 ff., where he says: "Facts are indifferent to Racine, as to Corneille or—we may add—to Molière. Beyond the theater, we find the

poetry. The story of Racine's art is the story of the clearing of the poet's imagination from the trammels of the theatrical technique previous to him."

12. V. Lugli, "Rileggendo Racine," in *La Cultura*, III (Rome, 1924), 492.
13. The care Racine took with his historical data can be seen from his *Préface*.
14. Jules Lemaître, *op. cit.*, p. 245.
15. See the *Préface*.
16. I note belatedly that Mario Fubini, too, in *Jean Racine e la critica delle sue tragedie*, p. 87, assumes an inner connection between Eriphile and Phèdre: "And one can also discern in the person of Eriphile a foreshadowing of Phèdre."
17. *Op. cit.*, pp. 252 ff.
18. Ferd. Lotheissen, *Geschichte der französischen Literatur im 17. Jahrhundert*, 2nd ed. (Vienna, 1894), II, 394.
19. In my little book *Sprache als Schöpfung und Entwicklung* (Heidelberg, 1905), pp. 73 ff., I have tried to analyze completely the surging beauty of his rhythms, so full of feeling.
20. *Oeuvres*, III, 557.
21. *Oeuvres* V, 208 and 211.
22. David Koigen, *Der moralische Gott* (Berlin, 1922), p. 175.
23. V. Imbriani, *Fame usurpate*, 3rd edn. (Bari, 1912), pp. 115 ff.
24. M. Fubini, *Jean Racine e la critica*, pp. 102 f.
25. Hegel, *Begriff der Religion*, ed. Lasson (Leipzig, 1925), p. 283.

CHAPTER 4

1. Boileau, *L'art poétique*, III.
2. *Oeuvres*, VI, 218–265.
3. Racine himself translated some of these works; *Oeuvres*, V, 477 ff.
4. *Epistola a Don Félix Quijado y Riquelme.*
5. *L'art poétique*, III.
6. See Piero Pizzo, *Die französische Tragödie der ersten Hälfte des 17. Jahrhunderts im Urteil ihrer Zeitgenossen* (diss. Zürich, 1914). Even Jules de la Mesnardière, who, in his *Poétique* (Paris, 1640), points emphatically to Euripides, shows only a theoretical and pedantic concept of tragedy. For details see

G. Lanson, *Esquisse d'une histoire de la tragédie française* (New York, 1920).

7. *Pensées*, ed. Brunschvicg (Paris, 1897–1904), p. 41.
8. *Ibid.*, p. 2.
9. *Oeuvres*, VI, 299 ff. and 318 ff.
10. Wolf Aly, *Geschichte der griechischen Literatur* (Leipzig, 1925), p. 73.
11. See Paul Zucker, *Die Theaterdekoration des Barock* (Berlin, 1925).
12. Quoted from E. Rigal, *Le théatre français avant la période classique* (Paris, 1901), p. 291.
13. J. E. Spingarn, *A History of Literary Criticism in the Renaissance*, 1st edn. (New York, 1899).
14. *Histoire de la littérature française*. Lanson also shows that this striving after simplified and stronger action was already to be noted in the works of Alexandre Hardy (*Hommes et livres* [Paris, 1895], p. 107).
15. *La Critica*, XVIII (Bari, 1920), 12 ff.
16. See his "Discourse before the Académie Francaise . . . January 2, 1685," *Oeuvres*, IV, 365 ff. One can perceive from it how clearly Racine recognized conditions in the theater, and Corneille's work: "You, Monsieur, who not only were his brother, but who also followed the same career for a long time—you know how indebted our poetry is to him; you know the state in which the French stage was when he commenced work. What disorder! What irregularity! No taste, no knowledge of the true beauties of the theater; the authors as ignorant as the spectators; the majority of the themes of plays extravagant and devoid of probability; no manners or morals; no characters; the diction still more defective than the plot, its main adornment being puns and miserable plays on words; in a word, all the rules of the art, even decency and propriety, violated everywhere.

"... What nobility, what skilled management of the themes! What vehemence of the passions! What gravity of the sentiments! What dignity, and at the same time what prodigious variety in the characters! How many kings, princes, and heroes of all nations he has presented to us! And always as they should be, always true to character, and never one like another! And with all that, a magnificence of expression befitting the masters of the world, whom he often portrays;

yet he is capable, when he wishes, of being humble and descending to the simplest and most naïve comedy, and in this too he still remains inimitable. In short, his most individual characteristic is a certain force, a certain sublimity which surprises and carries one away, and renders his faults—if indeed one could reproach him with having any—more estimable than the virtue of others."

17. *Op. cit.*, p. 25.

Chapter 5

1. *Oeuvres,* IV, 9 ff.
2. *Oeuvres,* VI, 33.
3. *Odyssey,* I, 32 ff.; after the Ger. tr. by Rudolf Alexander Schroder (Leipzig, 1911).
4. *Ibid.*, XIV, 57.
5. "Remarques sur l'Odyssée," *Oeuvres,* VI, 60.
6. *Odyssey,* V, 445 ff.
7. "Remarques," pp. 107 ff.
8. *Ibid.*, p. 125.
9. *Ibid.*, p. 159.
10. *Ibid.*, p. 114.
11. *Ibid.*, p. 120.
12. Details in the careful essays "De la langue de Racine" by Marty-Laveaux and "Etude sur le style de Racine" by Paul Mesnard, *Oeuvres,* VIII, i–xviii and xix–lxx.
13. *Oeuvres,* VI, 102 ff. and 125 ff.
14. *Ibid.*, p. 163.
15. G. Truc, *Le cas Racine* (Paris, 1921), p. 112.
16. Details in Ferd. Brunot, *Histoire de la langue française,* III (Paris, 1909), 241 ff.
17. Although Corneille's *Cid* was written seventeen years before Cyrano de Bérgérac's *Agrippine,* it marks the higher and, in a certain sense, later stage in dramatic art.

Index

Abrégé de l'histoire de Port-Royal (Racine), 32–34, 139
Académie Française
  Racine as member of, 17, 139
  Racine's discourse before, Jan. 2, 1685, quoted, 148–49
Académie Royale des Inscriptions et Médailles ("Petite Académie"), 16, 17, 139
Aeschylus, 107, 110
Aesthetics, Racine's attitude in the matter of, 129
Agnès de Saint-Thècle, Soeur (aunt), 11
Agrippine (Cyrano de Bérgérac), 129–30, 149
Alexandre Le Grand (Racine), 11, 48–49, 72, 139, 146
Alexandrines of Racine, 37, 134
Amphitryon (Kleist), 37
Andromaque (Racine), 20, 49–54, 72, 86, 117, 139, 146
Antiquity, the theater of, 112–13
Ariosto, Lodovico, 23, 127
Aristophanes, 37, 54
Aristotle, 107, 112, 115, 139
Arnauld, Antoine, 28, 109
Arnauldian man, Racine's portrayal of, 135
Art poétique (Boileau), 120
Athalie (Racine), 20, 39, 43–44, 85, 86, 87, 92–101, 102, 103, 128, 139, 145

Bains de Vénus, Les (Racine), 138
Bajazet (Racine), 20, 54, 57–61, 71, 72, 139
Baroque period, 26, 43, 71, 73, 106, 110, 114, 129
Bérénice (Racine), 57, 61–71, 72, 75, 86, 110, 117, 139
  and Corneille's *Tite et Bérénice*, 61–65, 146

Bérénice de Racine, La (Michaut), 146
Biblical plays of Racine's later period, 20
see also Athalie and *Esther*
Boileau-Despréaux, Nicholas, 7, 10, 12, 14, 15, 17, 105, 107, 120, 139, 142, 147
Bourgeois realism of Racine, 14
Britannicus (Racine), 57–61, 71, 72, 139

Calderón de la Barca, Pedro, 40
Calvin, John, 27, 109
Cantiques spirituel, Les, 30–31, 101–3
Cartesian man, Corneille's portrayal of, 135
Cervantes, Miguel de, 23
Champeslé, actress, 13–14, 117
Chapelain décoiffé (Racine, *et al.*), 139
Characters in Racine dramas, 36–37, 39, 40–41, 43, 135
Children of Racine
father role of Racine, 21–22
his concern for future of, 20
Christian community, Racine's devotion to, 7
Christian drama of Middle Ages, 113–14
Chute de Phaéton, La, Racine's libretto for, 20, 139, 143
Cid (Corneille), 130, 149
Classical authors
Racine's attitude toward, 126
rules of syntax and, 128
Comedy, Racine's writing of, 54–57
Commedia dell'arte, 119
Confessional poetry, 31
Conforming to popular image of the poet, Racine's lack of, 23
"Conversion" of Racine in reconciliation with Port-Royal, 12, 19, 20, 142
Corneille, Pierre, 14, 23, 36, 39, 45, 47, 48, 61–65, 73, 105, 106, 115, 119, 130–32, 134–35
Counter Reformation
French part in, 24–25
piety of, 26
Court circles
Racine in, 16–17
withdrawal from, 19, 20
Croce, Benedetto, 115, 116, 117
Cyrano de Bérgérac, Savinien, 129–30, 149

Dante, Alighieri, 23, 111
Death of Racine, 20–21
his attitude at the end, 22
"De la langue de Racine" (Marty-Laveaux), 149
Descarte, René, 109
Destiny, in Racine dramas, 39
Dionysus, and the theater of antiquity, 112–13
Discours de la Tragédie (Sarasin), 114
Dodart, Denis, 32
Domestic life of Racine, 21–22
Drama, Racine's renuncia-

tion of, *see* Renunciation of drama
Dramas of Racine, *see* Works of Racine
Du Parc, actress, 13–14, 117

Epigrams of Racine pouring scorn on work of some dramatists, 20
Escape from himself, Racine's constant efforts to, 7
Esther (Racine), 39, 43–44, 85–91, 101, 102, 103, 117, 133–34, 139, 145
"Etude sur le style de Racine" (Mesnard), 149
Euripides, 28, 45, 76, 79, 107, 109, 110, 111, 116, 126
Existence of evil, Racine's difficulty in accepting, 29

Failure, in some guise, in all of Racine dramas, 43, 44
Faith of Racine
core of, 28
in enduring bonds between human hearts, 38
Family
Racine's devotion to, 7, 20, 21
Racine's regard of family ties, 38
see also Children of Racine
Fate, in Racine dramas, 39, 47
Faust (Goethe), 101
First successes of Racine at court and in theater, 11
Francis de Sales, Saint, 25, 26, 144
French avoidance of the everyday in literary language, Racine's attitude on, 128
French stage of Racine's day, 105–6
Friendship, Racine's faithfulness in and need for, 10
Fubini, Mario, 102, 111, 146, 147

Gaining perception of Racine's quality through the senses, 36
Gallant eroticism, Racine reproached for, 39
Gentilhomme du Roy, Racine as, 17
Goethe, Johann von, 23, 66, 101, 111, 136
Grammatical rules, Racine's attitude toward, 128–29
Grandparents, Racine, as orphan, reared by, 8
Great Theater of the World, The, (Calderón), 40
Greek tragedy, and Racine, 28, 47, 106–7, 109–11, 112
Gundolf, F., 37

Hegel, Georg F. W., 102, 147
"Histoire du règne de Louis le Grand," Racine's work on, 14, 139
Historiographe du Roy, Racine as, 14–15, 139
Holy orders, Racine's consideration of taking of, 9, 19
Homer, 124–26, 127

Hugo, Victor, 123
Human relations, importance of, to Racine, 10

Ideas that dominated his time, Racine imbued with, 23
Idylle sur la Paix (Racine), 20, 139
Illusion comique (Corneille), 120
Imagination, absence of play of, in Racine, 23
Imbriani, V., 101, 147
Impromtu plays of *commedia dell'arte*, 119
Interests of Racine's countrymen and of his time, 24
Introduction à la vie dévote (St. Francis de Sales), 25
Iphigenia in Tauris (Goethe), 66
Iphigénie (Racine), 71–76, 77, 139
"Iphigénie en Tauride," Racine's prose draft of, 19, 122, 139

J. Racine e la critica delle sue tragedie (Fubini), 146, 147
Jansenism, 26, 27
  medieval type of monasticism in, 27
  practice of the contemplative life in, 27
  predestination, doctrine of, 27–28
  prejudice of Louis XIV against, 18, 34
  Racine's dual relationship with, 28–31, 32
Jansenist upbringing of Racine, 8
Jansenistic man, Racine's portrayal of, 135
Jean Racine (Lemaître), 146

Kleist, Heinrich von, 37
Koigen, David, 147

Lafayette, Madame de, 62
La Fontaine, Jean de, 8, 23, 132, 139
Lanson, Gustave, 32, 115, 116, 148
Le cas Racine (Truc), 142, 149
Lemaître, Jules, 57, 78, 146
Lettre à l'auteur des Imaginaires (Racine), 29, 139
Lettre aux deux apologistes de l'auteur des Imaginaires (Racine), 139
Le Vasseur, Abbé, 9, 10, 13, 123
Linguistic purism, Racine's attitude toward, 128–29
Literary fame of Racine, and his feelings about it, 14
Lotheissen, Ferd, 87, 147
Louis XIV
  address of Racine to the Academy on the glories of, 15–16
  on hearing *cantique* of Racine, 31
  prejudice of, against Jansenism, 18, 34
  Racine in court circles of, 16–17

Racine incurs displeasure of, 18, 20
Racine on, in his *Histoire* of Port-Royal, 34
Racine's *Alexandre* as work of homage to, 48
Racine's reading aloud to, 17
Racine's service to the state under, 7, 14–17, 20
Loyalty of Racine to the Church and the King, 18
Lugli, V., 147
Luther, Martin, 27, 109

Maintenon, Madame de, 17, 18, 31, 90
Malherbe, François de, 9, 141
Man as Godlike and as human, Racine's portrayal of, 42
Marly-le-Roi, Racine at, with the King, 17, 143
Material life, Racine's capacity for ennobling of, 23–24
Memoirs (Louis Racine), 19
Memory, astounding quality of Racine's, 123
Mesnard, Paul, 20, 92, 141, 149
Michaut, G., 146
Milton, John, 111
Mithridate (Racine), 54, 71–76, 139
Modest person, Racine as, 13
Molière, 23, 37, 119, 139
Montespan, Madame de, 17, 19, 143
Mörike, Eduard, 38
Moralische Gott, Der (Koigen), 147
Mort de Pompée, La (Corneille), 48, 146

Negative action, Racine's art of extracting drama from, 61
Nicole, Pierre, Racine's reply to derogatory pamphlet of, 11–12
Nymphe de la Seine, La (Racine), 138

Odes in praise of Port-Royal, by Racine, 138
Odyssey (Homer), 124–26, 127
Oeuvres de J. Racine (Mesnard, ed.), 141–49
Olympic Odes (Pindar), 124

Pascal, Blaise, 28, 109, 110
Pascalian man, Racine's portrayal of, 135
Passionateness, Racine's distrust and disapproval of, 13
Pensées (Pascal), 110
Petite Académie, Racine as member of, 16, 17
Phèdre (Racine), 19, 39, 72, 76–85, 86, 139
Philological pedantry, Racine's dislike of, 123
Pindar, 124
Plaideurs, Les (Racine), 43, 54–57, 119, 126, 139, 146
Planning a drama, Racine's method of, 123

Plato, 139, 143
Plutarch, 17, 111
Poet of renunciation, Racine as, 24, 86, 128
Poet of the unpoetical, Racine as, 23
Poeta philologue, Racine not to be regarded as, 111
Poetical language of Racine, 127
Poetics (Aristotle), 107
Poetry of Racine, 43, 126
Port-Royal
  disagreement of Racine with, and scoldings received from, 10–11
  odes of Racine in praise of, 138
  Racine's break with, 12
  Racine's history of, 32–34
  Racine's reconciliation with, 12
  Racine's spiritual home in, 109
  school days of Racine in, 8–9
Preciosity of language of classical tragedy, 129–31
Predestination, doctrine of, 27–28
  Racine's belief in, 28, 110, 111
Pride, Racine's hatred of, 13
Princesse de Clèves (Madame de Lafayette), 62
"Pseudo classicism" as phrase used for Racine's art, 40
Pseudo-intellectual "smartness," Racine's hatred of, 13
Racine, Jean Baptiste (son), 8, 21
Racine, Louis (son), 8, 17, 19, 21, 22, 143
Redemption of mankind as motive in medieval drama, 113
Religious aspects of Racine's works, 102
Religious determinism of Racine, 28–29, 111
Religious drama, history of, 40–41, 108–9
"Remarques sur Athalie" (Racine), 93
"Remarques sur l'Odyssée" (Racine), 149
Renommée aux Muses, La (Racine), 139
Renunciation
  as deepest emotion in Racine's plays, 61
  Racine as poet of, 24, 86, 128
Renunciation of drama by Racine, 7, 8, 19, 20, 101
  his son Louis quoted on, 19
  his literary works produced after, 19–20
Responsibility, Racine's deep sense of, 22
"Rileggendo Racine" (Lugli), 147
Rotrou, Jean Jacques, 45, 106, 134
Royal historiographer to Louis XIV, Racine as, 14–15, 139

Saint-Simon, Duc de, 20, 141

School days of Racine in Port-Royal, 8–9
Scudéry, Georges de, 116
Secrecy of Racine about his early scandalous literary tastes, 9
Secularism, Racine as child of, 23
Seignelay, Marquis de, 20
Self-examination motif, evoked by failure, in Racine dramas, 44, 45, 86
Seneca, 45, 76, 79, 110, 112, 116, 125, 126
Sexual love, Racine's appraisal of, 38–39
Shakespeare, William, 36, 117
Society as a supratemporal reality, Racine's concept of, 38
Sophocles, 28, 37, 107, 109, 110, 111
Spanish mystics, 109
Speech and action in Racine's dramas, 122–23, 127, 128
Split personality, Racine not a victim of, 31
Sprache als Schöpfung und Entwicklung (Vossler), 147
Stage successes of Racine, and his feelings about them, 14
Stances à Parthénice (Racine), 128, 138
Stereotyped theatrical conventions of Racine's day, 121
Style of Racine
  compared to that of Corneille, 134–35
  remnants of Corneille in, 132
Sur la convalescence du Roi (Racine), 139
Symposium (Plato), Racine's translation of, 139
Syntax, rules of
  classical authors and, 128
  Racine's attitude toward, 128–29

Tallemant, Abbé, 12
Tasso, Torquato, 66
Theater, Racine's renunciation of, *see* Renunciation of drama
Theater material that is exotic and strange, 105
Thebaïde, La (Racine), 11, 39, 44–47, 49, 71–72, 128, 138
Theocritus, 127
Tite et Bérénice (Corneille), 61–65, 146
Tragedies of Racine, deserving of closer study, 135–36
Tragic drama
  Christian drama of Middle Ages, 113–14
  dramas of Corneille, 115–16, 117
  dramas of Racine, 112, 116–18
  French stage of Racine's day, 105–6
  Greek tragic dramatists, and Racine, 28, 47, 106–7, 109–11, 112
  Racine's elevating of public taste in, 106–7

theater of antiquity, 112–13
theaters of Europe, about 1600, 114–15
Translation of Racine's verse, loss in, 35–36
Trésorier de France, Racine as, 17
Truc, Gonzague, 142, 149

"Umanismo, Teatro, Poesia nell'opera di Jean Racine" (Fubini), 146
Untruthfulness, Racine's feeling about, 9
Uzès, Racine's living with uncle in, 9, 10, 13

Vaugelas, Claude Favre de, 128
Vega, Lope de, 107, 117
Virgil, 23, 123, 126
Voltaire, 36, 64
Vossler, Karl, 147

Will of Racine, 32, 145
Withdrawal of Racine from court life and public life, 19, 20
Words, intellectual and ethical meanings of, in Racine's language, 132–33
Works of Racine
simplicity and clarity of, 35
special nature of, 35–42
value of, 42–44
see also individual titles of dramas

Youthful letters of Racine, classical literary quotations in, 123